IMMUNOLOGY

IMMUNOLOGY

FROM PASTEUR TO THE SEARCH FOR AN AIDS VACCINE

BY MARTIN J. GUTNIK

Franklin Watts
New York / London / Toronto / Sydney
A Venture Book 1989

Library of Congress Cataloging-in-Publication Data

Gutnik, Martin J.
Immunology : from Pasteur to the search for an AIDS vaccine / by
Martin J. Gutnik.
p. cm. — (A Venture book)
Bibliography: p.
Includes index.
Summary: A history of immunology from the discovery of
microorganisms with the invention of the microscope to the
development of vaccines for treating diseases.
ISBN 0-531-10672-1
1. Immunology—Popular works. [1. Immunology.] I. Title.
QR181.7.G87 1989
616.07′9—dc19   88-31372 CIP AC

to Adolph
Rosenblatt
friend
artist
scholar

Many thanks to
my good friend
Arthur Yaillen,
microbiologist,
for his help
in compiling
research for
this book

CONTENTS

IMMUNOLOGY

The Greek historian Thucydides caught the plague when it swept through the city of Athens in 430 B.C. He observed that those who were stricken by the disease but survived it, were never attacked by it again.

1

THE EARLY YEARS

In 430 B.C.E. (before the common era), a deadly disease spread through the city of Athens. Thucydides (460?–400? B.C.E.), the Greek historian, in referring to what we now suspect was a typhus epidemic, wrote that most of the population evacuated the city, leaving the caring of the sick to those who had had the disease and recovered. He said that these people were "free of apprehension," of getting the disease again. "No one was ever attacked a second time with the fatal insult."

The ancients understood that disease could be spread from one person to another. Although they had no knowledge of the nature of the disease, its cause, how it spread, or its cure, they did know about immunity. Once a person had suffered an onslaught of a *contagious* disease and survived, that person was seen as incapable of becoming reinfected with the same disease. The person was said to be *immune,* from the Latin word *immunis,* "exempt from changes."

Mithridates the Great, king of Pontus (120?–63 B.C.E.), supposedly attempted to protect himself from poisons by drinking the blood of ducks that had been treated with the same poisons. He inferred that the ducks' blood would strengthen his system and render him immune to these *virulent* chemicals.

Other people did such bizarre things as eat the livers of mad dogs to protect themselves from the dreaded disease rabies. Although these wild attempts at immunization did not work, there was some soundness in their reasoning: a little bit of poison would protect you against a big dose.

VARIOLATION

It was the awareness of immunity that, in the fifteenth century, brought people to attempt to induce immunity by inoculating well persons against the disease smallpox, which often scourged the populations of Europe.

The process of *variolation* was developed in the Middle East. Physicians took the infective fluid from pox *lesions* (diseased tissue), made a *serum* (liquid), and *inoculated* (introduced into the body) willing individuals, in an attempt to produce a limited infection. It was believed that this limited infection would then give the inoculated person immunity to the disease.

Variolation was introduced into Europe by Lady Mary Wortley Montague (1689–1762), an English writer.

While living in Constantinople, Lady Mary Wortley Montague followed the Turkish practice and had her son inoculated against smallpox. Later she tried to introduce the practice in England, but without success.

It had a very limited success. Quite often the person inoculated developed a serious case of the disease. Until the discovery of microorganisms, however, variolation was the best defense people had against the invisible killers.

THE INVENTION OF THE MICROSCOPE

Zacharias Janssen (c. 1590), a Dutch spectacle-maker, is credited with discovering the principle of the compound microscope. The first lenses were crude and cumbersome, yet they afforded the first glimpse into a world previously unseen—the world of *microorganisms*. The link between these minute creatures and disease was not realized immediately. Most observers used the microscope merely to classify the organisms they studied.

A German Jesuit living in Rome, Athanasius Kircher (1601–1680), was among these. Kircher first used simple lenses to study the makeup of plants. He saw the rectangular and oblong-shaped cells of these living organisms and called them *filaments*.

When the plague struck the city, Kircher turned his lenses to the actual study of disease. Although his tools were crude, when he studied the lesions of plague victims, Kircher was able to see wormlike structures. He wrote down what he saw, thus being the first person to record his observations of the plague *bacteria*.

The relationship of microorganisms to disease was clearly established by an Italian, Giovar Cosimo Bonomo (1666–1696). In 1687, Bonomo published a paper

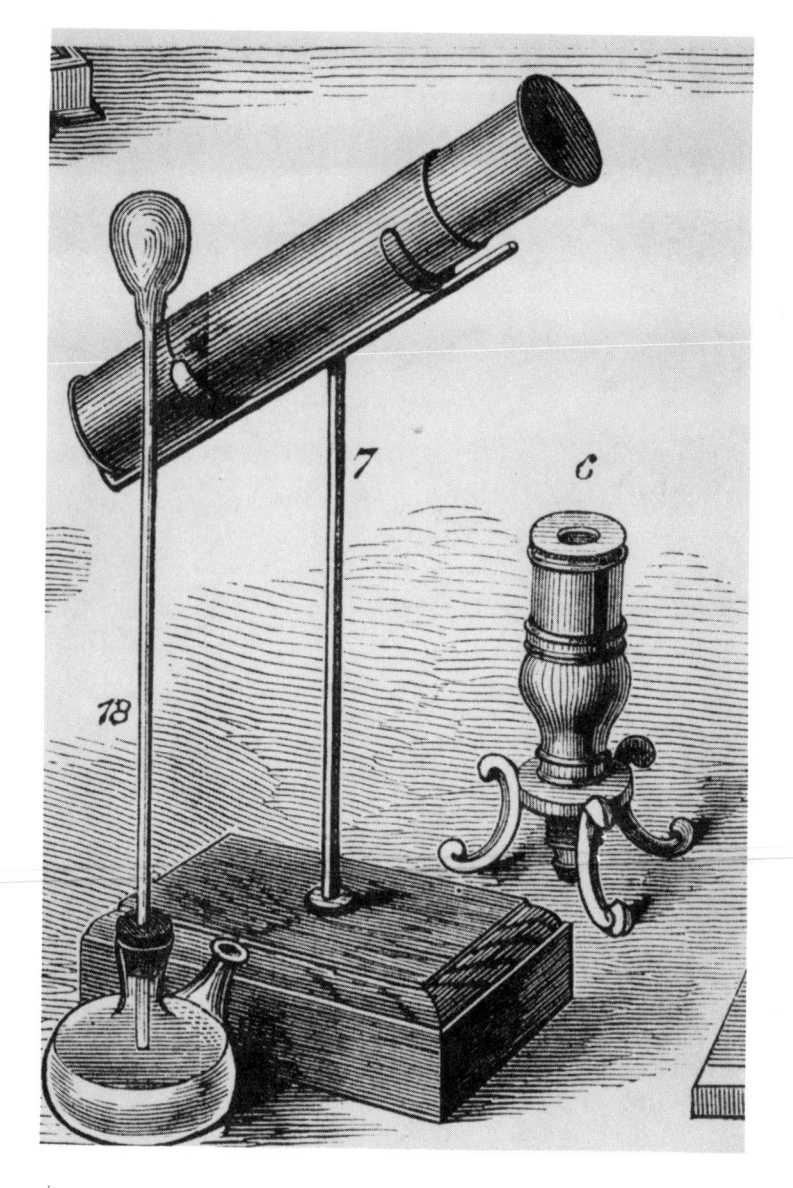

The compound microscope
of Zacharias Janssen is
shown here to the far right.

The German Jesuit Athanasius Kircher, through his studies with the microscope, came to believe that diseases were caused by invisible bodies.

in which he identified mites, very small insectlike animals similar to ticks, as the cause of the disease scabies.

Before Bonomo's discovery that scabies was caused by a mite that attached itself to the outer layer of the skin, the treatment for scabies was to take medicine internally. Bonomo pointed out that this medicine was useless, that the only effective treatment for scabies was external salves or cremes.

Bonomo's discovery was a breakthrough in medicine. He had demonstrated that knowing what causes a disease is the first step toward discovering how to treat and cure the disease. However, Bonomo's methods were mostly ignored by the scientific community. It was not until a century and a half later that scientists again linked microorganism with a disease of humans.

THE DISCOVERY OF BACTERIA

Antonie van Leeuwenhoek (1632–1723) was a cloth merchant in Delft, Holland. He also served as custodian for the town hall, a political appointment. His jobs gave him much free time to spend on his avocation, grinding lenses of powerful magnification for simple microscopes.

Because of his political ties, Leeuwenhoek had many influential friends, among them the physician Reiner de Graaf, the discoverer of the follicle that now bears his name; and Henry Oldenburg, secretary of the Royal Society of London, one of the most progressive scientific organizations of the time.

As early as 1674, van Leeuwenhoek, through his microscopes, was able to see creatures which, by description, were almost certainly bacteria. Patiently, the Dutch scientist spent his spare time looking through his crude microscopes. Here he saw a world previously unknown, a world of rods, spirals, and cones; a minute, moving symphony of globs of greens, grays, and browns. These globs, the larger microorganisms, were, in fact, algae, protozoa, and yeasts; the rods, cones, and spirals were bacteria.

Van Leeuwenhoek was an avid experimenter. He would prick his finger and study his own blood under these crude lenses. Here he saw *erythrocytes* (red blood cells). He scraped the back of his teeth with an instrument and studied the matter he removed. It was about this matter from the back of his teeth that he wrote to Oldenburg at the Royal Society: "There were many small living animalcules. . . ."

These "animalcules" were actually bacteria. Van Leeuwenhoek wrote about them, diagramed them, and described their movements. But his observations had little impact on the scientific community because he was secretive about his lenses. Other scientists of the time did not see what van Leeuwenhoek did.

Van Leeuwenhoek's research, however, did stimulate others to study microscopic forms of life. Because the Dutchman's simple lenses were unavailable, the work was done with compound microscopes, derived from Zacharias Janssen. Using the scientific method, these scientists studied and classified a variety of microorganisms. They wrote of the microorganisms' relationships to life processes and to disease.

*Antonie van Leeuwenhoek made
simple microscopes through which
he observed microorganisms.*

THE THEORY OF SPONTANEOUS GENERATION (ABIOGENESIS)

With the discovery of microorganisms and the further development of the compound microscope, medicine was at the doorstep to giant advances in the control of disease, but there remained many questions to be answered. Certain controversies between the scientific scholars of the time had to be resolved. One of these major disagreements was the argument over spontaneous generation.

Spontaneous generation, or *abiogenesis,* is the belief that living *organisms* can be produced from nonliving matter or decomposing *organic* matter. The scientific community was split, those opposing the theory arguing that life can only come from life.

As far back as the Greek philosopher Aristotle (384– 322 B.C.E.), some great thinkers believed in spontaneous generation. Aristotle himself said: "any dry thing which becomes humid and any humid thing which dries produces animals." These thoughts were stimulated by observations of worms in feces and other decomposing organic matter.

Many scientists believing in spontaneous generation went further than Aristotle. In the 1600s, the Flemish physician and chemist Jan Baptista van Helmont (1580–1644) put forward a recipe for the spontaneous generation of mice from grain.

It was Francesco Redi (1626–1697), an Italian physician, who first refuted the theory of spontaneous generation with hard, scientific evidence. Redi had difficulty believing that living things could arise out of dead organic matter. To prove his theories, he performed the following experiment.

Redi cooked some raw meat to make certain any microorganisms it contained would be killed. He put this cooked meat into three labeled containers. The first container was left uncovered and exposed to the air; the second was covered with a fine sterile gauze and sealed at the edges; and the third was completely sealed with heavy parchment.

Redi theorized that the container covered with gauze would attract flies because the odor of the meat would escape and rise in the air, but the flies would not be able to enter the container. He thought that the parchment-sealed container would not attract flies because no odor could escape into the outside air.

Redi's hypothesis was that the meat in the uncovered container would attract flies and that flies would lay eggs on the meat; then, after a time, maggots would appear. Thus, he postulated, it would prove that maggots came from the flies and not from the meat.

Redi observed the three containers over a period of time, logging the results of what happened in each jar. He observed that flies landed on the meat for a considerable period of time and then flew away. After several weeks, maggots appeared on this meat.

Some flies landed on the gauze of the second container and remained there for some time. They could not enter the container to land on the meat. Several weeks later, maggots appeared on the gauze covering of the second container, but not on the meat inside.

Flies did not even attempt to land on the parchment-sealed container. Throughout the experiment, this container was free of maggots.

After several repetitions of this experiment, Redi concluded that, since only the first container had maggots on the meat, the maggots appeared as a direct result of the flies being on the meat. This is also why there were maggots on the gauze of the second container and no maggots on or in the third. Thus, Redi reasoned that maggots come from flies, not from decaying organic material. His experiments partially proved life comes from like forms of life.

Redi proved that the worms in meat were the larvae from flies, not mysterious manifestations from an unknown source. Redi also observed that there were male and female flies, and that the females laid the eggs.

Although Redi's experiments were impressive, the scientific community still was not convinced. Many scientists said that what Redi proved may be true for flies, but not for *microbes* (microscopic organisms).

In 1750, a Catholic priest in England named John Needham, despite Redi's findings, presented a scientific

The Italian physician Francesco Redi, through his experiments, presented strong evidence against the theory of spontaneous generation.

paper that supported the belief that microorganisms arose spontaneously from spoiled broth. Needham boiled meat broth in flasks, sealed them, and then let them stand for awhile. Upon examination with a microscope, microorganisms could be found within the broth.

Needham took this to be proof that these organisms arose from the broth. He stated that if the microorganisms had been in the broth before boiling, the boiling would have killed them.

An Italian physiologist, Lazzaro Spallanzani (1729–1799), studied Needham's findings and then released the results of his own experiments, which refuted those of Needham. Spallanzani's investigations were on the same tack as those of Needham. The difference in the findings was in the process of the investigation.

Spallanzani boiled the broth for a longer period of time and then sealed the flasks instantly, so that no air could be drawn back into the flasks. When he found no microorganisms in the broth, he concluded that the theory of spontaneous generation was in error. Needham was still unconvinced.

The controversy continued for many years, with a number of scientists offering their work in support of either Needham or Spallanzani, until Louis Pasteur (1822–1895) ended it for good.

Pasteur boiled broth in long-necked flasks and then, after boiling, let the flasks stand unsealed. Afterward, the broth in these flasks remained free of microorganisms. The microorganisms in the air entered the flasks, but settled on the long necks of the flasks instead of in the broth. Pasteur then demonstrated that the microorganisms in the air were the same as those on the necks of the flasks. He concluded that there never were micro-organisms arising from the broth; they were already present in the air, and only used the broth as a source of nutrition.

Pasteur's findings put to rest any argument in support of spontaneous generation and released the minds of science to move forward to greater discoveries.

2

THE BEGINNING OF A SCIENCE

On May 17, 1749, in Berkeley, Gloucestershire, England, one of the great names in immunology was born, Edward Jenner. As a young man, Jenner traveled to London, where he studied medicine at University College. After graduation, he practiced medicine and taught at his alma mater. Later he served as president of the Royal College of Physicians (1881–1888).

Jenner was an extremely competent and successful physician. He was also a keen observer and researcher. It was this gift of observation, in conjunction with the trained mind of the physician, that brought Jenner to his dramatic experiments with smallpox.

While treating patients for smallpox in his practice in Gloucestershire, Jenner recalled a young girl who had once told him she could not catch smallpox because she had had *cowpox*. This recollection now interested Jenner, as well as did the work of Lady Mary Wortley Montague (see page 13).

Jenner found that there were many instances of people, mainly farmers, who had been infected with cowpox and had never contracted smallpox. Acting on this research, Jenner began to experiment. He extracted some fluid from cowpox lesions (sores) on the arm of a milkmaid, Sarah Nelmes. Using this fluid to make a serum, he then inoculated a boy, James Phipps, and then several other people in his village.

Jenner conducted his experiment according to the scientific procedures of his time. He made two cuts on each person's arm and introduced the cowpox virus into the bloodstream. Each inoculated person then became infected with cowpox. Approximately six weeks later, Jenner inoculated the same people with the smallpox virus, but it had no effect on them.

Jenner performed his dramatic experiments in 1796. In 1798, he presented his findings to the Royal Society of London, in a paper entitled "An Inquiry into the Causes and Effects of the Variolae Vaccinae." The Fellows of the Society were skeptical of the boldness of his experiments and their variance from standard forms of practice. Despite their skepticism, Jenner continued his research. In 1799, he published another document entitled "Further Observations on the Variolae Vaccinae or Cowpox." Jenner's second paper convinced his peers, and his methods for preventing smallpox became accepted. Jenner had introduced vaccination to the world.

The word vaccination, from the Latin *vacca,* which

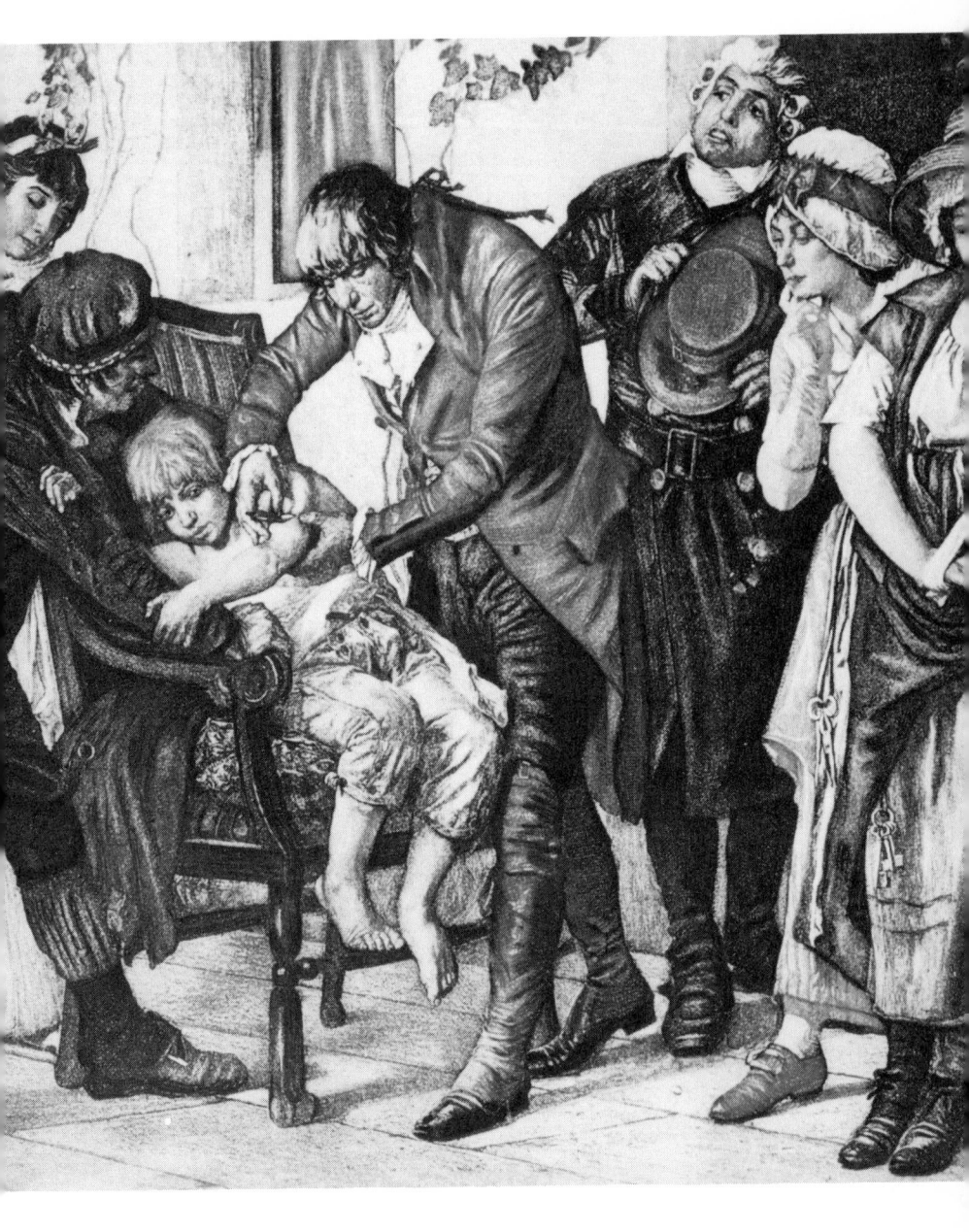

Edward Jenner vaccinating James Phipps

means "cow," is a method of stimulating immunity to an infectious disease by injection of the causative microorganism or its byproducts. Jenner's success was in using an *attenuated* (weakened) form of the smallpox virus in the form of the cowpox virus. Possibly, the human smallpox virus, over many years of passing from cow to cow, had become so weakened that it lost its ability to produce smallpox in people. Thus, when Jenner used the cowpox virus on humans, it caused these individuals' bodies to produce *antibodies* (proteins) that gave them immunity to the smallpox virus. Today scientists can clearly distinguish between the two viruses.

Jenner's vaccination was *active immunization*. In this process, a vaccinated person develops immunity to a *pathogen* because the vaccination causes the body to produce antibodies against the pathogen.

The profound effect of Jenner's discoveries was not realized until a hundred years later, when Louis Pasteur formulated his germ theory of disease. It was Pasteur's work that moved the science of immunology out of the era of observation and into the era of experimentation.

THE FATHER OF IMMUNOLOGY

Louis Pasteur was born on December 24, 1822, in Dole, a small town in France. His father, Jean-Joseph, was a tanner by profession and an ex-sergeant in Napoleon's army. After the Napoleonic campaigns across Europe, Jean-Joseph married and settled down. He and his wife had four children, three daughters and one son, Louis.

*Not until the nineteenth century was
vaccination in general use as protection
against smallpox. In this 1872 woodcut,
a Brooklyn doctor draws serum from a cow
to vaccinate waiting children in his parlor.*

The Pasteurs moved from Dole to Arbors, where Louis received his early education. He was a careful student who demonstrated a natural talent for art. He made numerous portraits in pencil and pastel of his family, friends, and surroundings. Although he loved art, Pasteur chose to pursue the study of science.

Pasteur was a serious student who concentrated almost totally on schoolwork and did not bother with the games or friendships of his classmates. He was very much a loner. He had one goal at this time in his life, and that was to graduate and become a teacher.

In 1848, Pasteur became a professor of physics and, in 1849, was appointed to the University of Strasbourg. Here he met and married Marie Laurent, the daughter of the rector of the university.

In 1854, Pasteur was appointed dean of the faculty of sciences at the University of Lille. It was at Lille, two years later, that Pasteur became interested in the activities of microorganisms, when a wine merchant commissioned him to find out why his wine was spoiling.

After studying the wine-making process, Pasteur concluded that germs (microbes) entered the wine while it was being made. One type of microbe, yeast, caused the wine to turn into alcohol. This was the desired result. Another type of microbe, bacteria, caused the wine to turn to acid and spoil.

Pasteur suggested that the undesirable bacteria could be killed by sterilization of the equipment used in the wine-making process. He also postulated that, by heating the wine itself, any remaining bacteria would be eliminated. This was a great breakthrough for the wine industry. Today, this heating process, known as pasteurization, is used not only in the making of wine, but in the sterilization of milk and many other products.

During the following years, Pasteur became involved in a number of projects that heightened his reputation in the scientific community. Among these was the disproof of the theory of spontaneous generation, in 1861 (see page 21).

In 1865, Pasteur began to work on the causes of pébrine, a disease that affected silkworms. After numerous experiments, he found that a particular microorganism present in diseased silkworms was not found in healthy ones. It was evident to him that the microorganism was the cause of the disease, and that a diseased silkworm would spread the infection to healthy worms.

Pasteur told the silk manufacturers that to prevent the microbe from infecting their worms, they must grow the worms under conditions that would prevent the infection. If they did this, then their stock would be disease-free.

The years that Pasteur fought the silkworm were difficult for him. During this time, his father and two of his daughters died. The scientist was grief-stricken. He lapsed into a deep depression, which led in turn to a nervous breakdown. Although one of Pasteur's legs became partially paralyzed as a result of the trauma, he eventually recovered and went on to save France's silkworm industry.

It was during this same period that Pasteur was called upon by French farmers to find a cure for chicken cholera. Pasteur began to experiment, and soon isolated the microorganism that caused the disease.

*Louis Pasteur dictating notes
to his wife during his research
on the disease of the silkworm*

Pasteur now asked himself a question that put him on the frontier of a breakthrough that would affect medicine for all the years to come: If we know what germs cause a particular disease, how then can we prevent the disease?

In his laboratory, Pasteur had some soup in which he had been keeping chicken-cholera bacteria. Perhaps, he thought, if these germs were injected into healthy chickens, the healthy chickens might be protected from getting the disease. He decided to test his theory.

After receiving the cholera bacteria, the healthy chickens became sick, but did not die. The scientist then exposed these vaccinated chickens to diseased chickens. The vaccinated chickens did not get the disease. It seemed to Pasteur that, once exposed to a weakened form of the germ, a chicken's blood had the ability to protect it from the deadly form of cholera.

The defeat of chicken cholera was a great victory for Pasteur. His prestige and reputation were riding high. He was next asked to find a cure for anthrax, a disease affecting sheep.

It seems that great scientific minds often work simultaneously. In his experimentations, a French scientist named Casimir Joseph Davaine (1812–1882) had discovered that the blood of dead sheep contained rod-shaped bacteria and that, when these bacteria were injected into the blood of healthy sheep, the sheep would come down with anthrax.

Pasteur took Davaine's research even further. He isolated the bacteria that seemed to cause anthrax in a *pure culture*, i.e., a culture obtained under *sterile* conditions and thereby free of all other microorganisms. He then transferred these bacteria into healthy sheep. These

34

sheep came down with the disease, thus proving, un-equivocally, that bacteria are capable of causing disease.

With the knowledge of Jenner's discoveries one hundred years earlier, Pasteur began to work on a method of attenuating the anthrax bacteria so that it could be made into a *vaccine*. He discovered that, by heating the bacteria at 42 to 43 degrees Celsius (76° to 77°F), the virulence was greatly reduced.

On May 2, 1882, in Melun, France, Pasteur tested his theory. He inoculated twenty-five sheep with his at-tenuated anthrax bacteria. Twenty-five other sheep, in a control group of fifty, were not inoculated. Afterward, all fifty sheep were inoculated with a virulent form of the anthrax bacteria. The twenty-five sheep that were not protected by the attenuated vaccine died, while the twenty-five that were vaccinated were not affected at all.

This was another great accomplishment for Pasteur. In memory of Jenner's work with cowpox and smallpox, Pasteur named the process of inoculating animals with an attenuated form of a germ, vaccination.

Pasteur believed in the *germ theory of disease*. He knew that different microorganisms caused different dis-eases. His work with chicken cholera and anthrax pre-pared him for experiments and research that would lead to his greatest accomplishment, a vaccine for rabies.

A YOUNG BOY
AND A MAD DOG

Rabies, also known as hydrophobia, is a disease of the central nervous system which affects animals much more frequently than people, and which can be spread from one warm-blooded animal to another through bites and inhalation. It is a deadly disease that, up until Pasteur, had no known cure. Perhaps Pasteur chose to work on this particular disease because he felt more qualified in animal medicine.

In 1879, a veterinarian named Galtier showed that rabies could be transmitted to other animals by inoculation of the saliva of a rabid animal. Pasteur, using Galtier's method, began his experiments by inoculating a rabbit with the mucus of a child who had died from rabies. Within a day and a half, the rabbit died. As in his successful study of anthrax and cholera, Pasteur looked for the *causative agent,* the microorganism that caused the disease. But he could not find it because the causative agent of rabies is a *virus* and not a bacterium. A virus is much smaller than a bacterium. The microscopes of the time were not powerful enough to reveal something so small.

Pasteur now attempted to find a new method of attenuating the microorganism. Suspecting that the causative agent was present in the saliva of rabid dogs he injected some of the saliva in the spinal cord of a live rabbit. Afterward, he removed the rabbit's spinal cord and dried it under sterile conditions. He made the serum for his vaccine from the dried-up spinal cord. He theorized that the vaccine, given in a series of injections, would prevent a bite victim from getting rabies.

It was not long after Pasteur began his experiments that an incident occurred that put him in a position to test his new vaccine on a human.

On July 6, 1885, a young boy, Joseph Meister, was bitten by a rabid dog. The family doctor said that, there

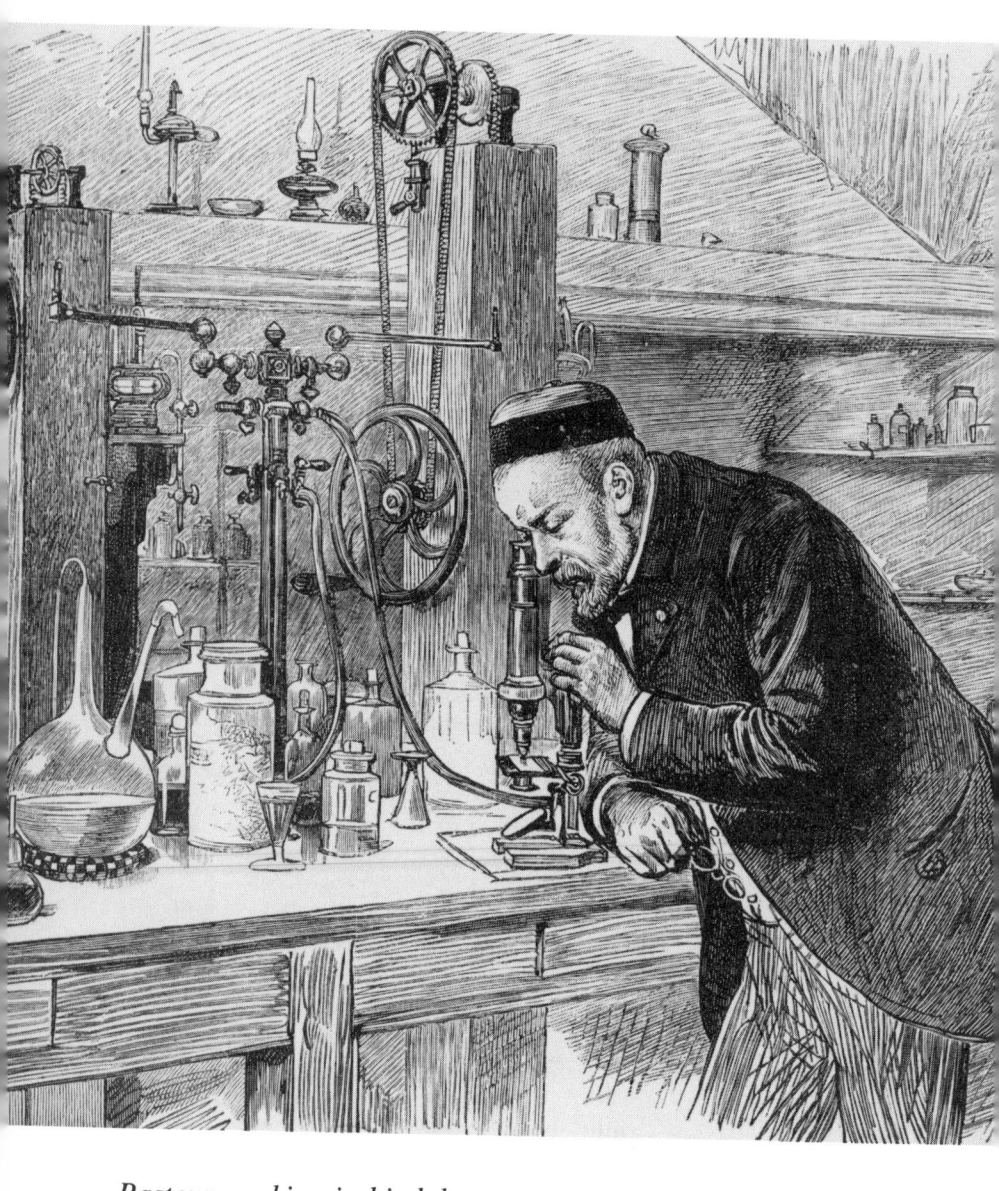

Pasteur working in his laboratory in 1885, the year he saved the life of a young boy, Joseph Meister

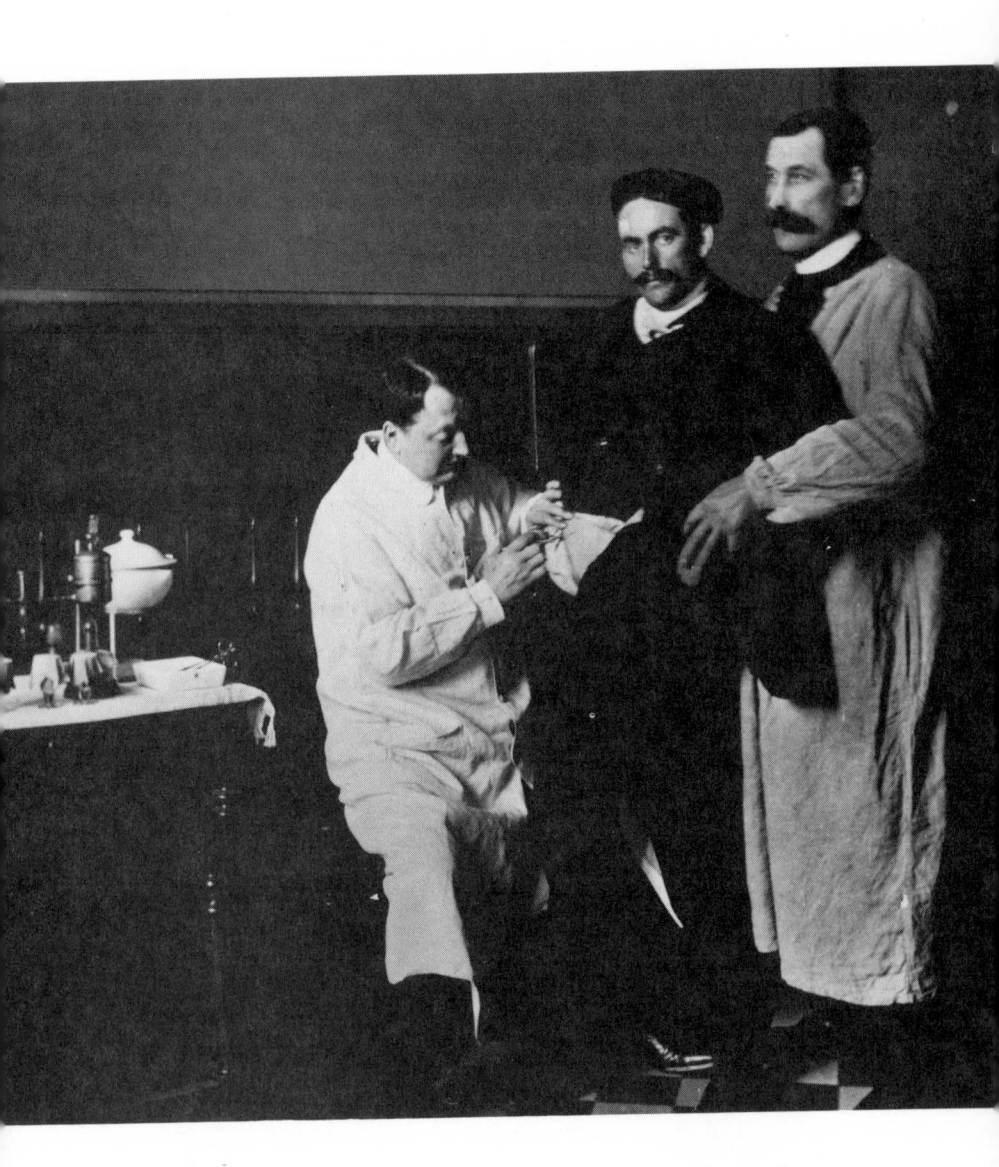

By the turn of the century, Pasteur's method of combating rabies was widely used. This photograph from about 1905 was taken at the Pasteur Institute in Paris. A man bitten by a mad dog is receiving an injection against rabies.

being no doubt the dog was rabid, the boy was bound to die. The mother, beside herself with grief, pleaded with the doctor to do something. The doctor, having read about Pasteur's work, told the mother that, if the boy had any hope, it would be with Pasteur's new experimental treatment.

The boy was brought to Pasteur, who gave him a series of injections of the attenuated rabies virus over a ten-day period. Each injection was a more powerful dose of the virus than the previous one.

Pasteur's vaccine proved successful; the boy lived. Joseph Meister became the first human being ever to be bitten by a rabid animal and known to survive. Pasteur reported the results of his work with Meister to the Academy of Science on October 26, 1885. The Academy and the world scientific community accepted the results without criticism.

Louis Pasteur died in 1895. His contributions to the fields of *microbiology* and immunology remain unsurpassed. Pasteur's curious mind and relentless search for answers to seemingly unanswerable questions led him to discoveries that tremendously benefited humanity. His epitaph: Joseph Meister lived.

3

FROM BACTERIA TO THE DISCOVERY OF ANTIBODIES

At the time of Pasteur, much work was being done in the fields of medical research and immunology by a host of scientists. It was an exciting time. People such as Joseph Lister (1827–1912) worked with developing the germ theory and aseptic systems for surgery and childbirth. Lionel S. Beale (1828–1906) wrote *The Microscope and Medicine,* a book about disease germs, in which he pointed out that bacteria and fungi could be found everywhere. Norwegian physician Armaur Hanser, in 1874, discovered the leprosy bacillus (a kind of bacteria), and the Englishman William Budd, in 1873, worked on the causes and control of typhoid fever and cholera.

These scientists followed precise methods as they

did their research and performed their experiments. They kept records of their discoveries in journals, and published articles defending their results. Methods and ideas were varied, but shared. They all learned from one another.

Much of Pasteur's work with viruses involved using cultures to make vaccines. In this aspect of his research, Pasteur owed much to a German bacteriologist named Robert Koch.

ROBERT KOCH
(1843–1910)

Robert Koch was born in Clausthal, Germany, the third child of thirteen children. His father, a mining inspector, was a hard worker and a strong believer in education.

Koch, like all his brothers and sisters, went to the gymnasium (a German secondary school) for his basic education, where he was a conscientious student, demonstrating an intense desire to learn about any subject. He did fairly well in school, showing a propensity for the sciences, so his parents sent him to the University of Göttingen for a medical education.

The university, located in a rural setting in Germany, was an institution whose faculty was dedicated to research. Students were encouraged to use a "hands-on" approach to their studies. Koch, among them, enthusiastically engaged in research. It was this training that established the foundation for the rest of Koch's career as a medical researcher.

After graduation, Koch settled in Wollstein as a general practitioner of medicine. When not seeing patients, he did research with his microscope.

Koch is best remembered for his work in obtaining pure cultures on solid media, material that bacteria grow on. Being able to obtain a pure culture was a giant

Koch's Postulates:
Methods for Identifying a
Disease-Causing Organism

1. The disease-causing organism must be found in all cases of the disease, must be in all lesions, and must be described in detail.

2. The disease-causing organism must be able to be isolated and grown in pure culture on artificial media.

3. The disease-causing organism must be able to be inoculated, in pure culture, into an experimental animal and produce the same disease in that animal.

4. When the experimental animal develops the disease, the disease-causing agent must be able to be recovered from the experimental animal. This agent will be exactly the same as the original disease-causing organism.

breakthrough in the isolation of the causative organisms of disease. It was not until Koch developed his pure-culture method that the germ theory of disease was finally accepted.

Koch also discovered the causative organisms of tuberculosis and cholera, two then deadly diseases. His research in tuberculosis led him to the development of standardized methods for systematically identifying the causative agent of a disease. This method of research, which later became known as Koch's postulates, is used to this day by researchers working with such diseases as cancer and AIDS.

Koch's contributions to the field of immunology and bacteriology made possible a great burst of research in the last two decades of the nineteenth century. It was during this period of time, 1880–1900, that most of the known disease-causing bacterial organisms were isolated and preventive measures instituted.

ÉMILE ROUX, ALEXANDRE YERSIN, EMIL VON BEHRING, SHIBASABURO KITASATO

Roux and Yersin were co-workers of Louis Pasteur. In Paris, France, in 1888, they helped to found the Pasteur Institute, a center for research in bacteriology, medicine, and microbiology. At the Institute, Roux and Yersin taught a course in microbiology. It was here that the two scientists discovered the bacterial *toxin* of the diphtheria bacillus.

*Robert Koch developed standardized methods
for identifying the causative agent of tuberculosis. Here he gives a demonstration of his
methods before his colleagues at the Psycho-
logical Gesselschaft in Berlin in 1882.*

Emil Behring and Shibasaburo Kitasato, expanding upon Roux and Yersin's discovery, experimented with the diphtheria bacillus. They discovered that an injection of the modified toxin into an animal induced the animal to develop a neutralizing material against the toxins and become immune. This immunity was directly ascribed to the development of these specific neutralizing substances, called *antitoxins*. An antitoxin is any substance which neutralizes a toxin. The discovery of antitoxins gave rise to the concept of antibodies. An antibody is a protein substance which neutralizes specific *antigens*.

Roux solved the problem of producing antitoxins on a large enough scale for human treatment. The antidiphtheric serum was first tried, with huge success, in two children's hospitals in Paris. In 1894, Roux presented the results of his experiments at the International Congress of Hygiene, in Budapest, Hungary, where it was received with much enthusiasm.

Meanwhile, in 1890, at the Koch Institute, in Berlin, Germany, Behring and Kitasato pursued their theory of antibody production. While working on the development of a tetanus antitoxin, they observed specific substances that they called antibodies. They saw that antibodies were able to neutralize toxins; *agglutinate* (clump) bacteria, thus rendering them harmless; kill and dissolve bacteria in the presence of normal serum; *opsonize* bacteria (help blood *phagocytes*, cells that eat bacteria); and sensitize the body to resist shock.

The discovery of diphtheria antitoxins was generally attributed to Behring. This brought him international acclaim. Students from many countries now came to the Koch Institute to work with him, and not Koch.

In 1896, Behring was made a nobleman, and his name was changed to von Behring. As he became part of the nobility, he also went into the business of manufacturing serum and vaccine. With money from this and other ventures, he bought real estate and became a well-to-do landowner. In 1901, Emil von Behring received the first Nobel Prize for Medicine for his work in *serotherapy* (passive immunity).

Passive acquired immunity is when a person acquires antibodies from another source. The person is not manufacturing his/her own antibodies but, rather, is borrowing them. This is a very fast-acting type of immunity, but of short duration.

4

THE BASIS OF IMMUNITY

With the discovery of antibodies, research in the field of immunology burgeoned. Medical scientists in many countries began to search for answers to the question, How do our bodily defenses function?

In the late nineteenth century, two opposing theories regarding the immune response were developed: the *cellular theory* (phagocytic theory) professed that the immune response was centered in cells called *phagocytes;* the *humoral theory* stated that the immune response was centered in the blood serum.

The disagreement persisted well into the twentieth century, with great scientific minds arguing for both sides. Finally, it was resolved that the immune response involves all factors that affect resistance to infectious disease, both cellular and humoral.

ÉLIE METCHNIKOFF
AND CELLULAR THEORY

Élie Metchnikoff was born in 1845 in the Ukraine. His father, Ilya, was a landowner, which enabled Metchnikoff to receive an education, a privilege afforded only the wealthy during those times.

Metchnikoff was a capricious child whose interests varied from music to nature study. At eight, he was taught botany by a tutor hired for his older brother. Soon Metchnikoff began to write lectures alone on the subject and read them to his peers.

Being an exceptional student, Metchnikoff was admitted to Kharkov University, where he studied biology. His fickle nature remained with him, as he transferred from Kharkov to a succession of universities in Europe. During this time, he studied zoology and biology.

Metchnikoff learned much from his European travels and, upon his return to Russia, went to St. Petersburg to earn a doctorate. He soon left St. Petersburg and went to Italy. He returned from Italy and went back to St. Petersburg. All the while, Metchnikoff studied marine life and invertebrates (animals without a backbone).

Metchnikoff married, but his wife died three years later of tuberculosis. In 1875, he married again. Olga, his new wife, was half his age. He seemed to now settle down a bit, and began teaching and researching at the University of Odessa. In 1881, Olga's parents died, leaving her a small fortune. Financially secure, Metchnikoff and his wife went to live in Messina, Italy, where the most important work of his life began, his work on *phagocytosis*.

One day, while working in his laboratory studying starfish larvae under the microscope, Metchnikoff postulated that these larvae might protect themselves from infection in a digestive manner, like the swelling about the wound in human skin. To test his theory, he stuck rose thorns into some of the larvae. The next day the thorns were surrounded by amoeboid cells, cells that rushed to surround the wound to protect the starfish against harmful intruders.

Metchnikoff became extremely excited over his observations. This starfish experiment formed the axis of his phagocyte theory. According to this theory, all animals have cellular reactions to protect their bodies against infection. Metchnikoff theorized that these cells would challenge any foreign invader; they were the body's major defense against bacterial infections. Metchnikoff published his findings in 1882.

After his initial discovery, Metchnikoff returned to Russia, where he began a series of experiments with daphnia (water fleas). In these researches, he discovered that the daphnia had phagocytic cells that could ingest and destroy specific yeasts harmful to the crustacean. In 1884, he published a paper on these studies entitled "A Yeast Disease of Daphnia, a Contribution to the Theory of the Struggle of Phagocytes against Pathogens."

After his paper on daphnia, Metchnikoff experienced worldwide acclaim. Scientists from many countries came to study with the Russian eccentric.

Metchnikoff spent the rest of his life studying the process of phagocytosis in higher animals. In 1908, he won the Nobel Prize in medicine for his contributions to the field of immunology.

*The Russian bacteriologist
Élie Metchnikoff in his laboratory*

OPPOSING THEORIES

Metchnikoff's theories on phagocytosis were influenced by other scientists working on related theories. Koch and others observed that pathogenic bacteria were found in the blood *leukocytes* (white cells). This was a significant observation, but none of these scientists carried their research further. It was not until years later that the significance of this discovery was understood.

Other researchers suggested that leukocytes play an important part in the body's defenses against disease, specifically bacterial disease. Experiments were performed in which leukocytes were observed engulfing foreign particles. This was a significant observation in support of the phagocyte theory.

In spite of the mounting evidence that phagocytic cells were the main line of the body's defensive system, there were still many important scientists who disagreed with Metchnikoff and his supporters. These researchers believed that the body's main line of defense was in the blood serum, not in the cells. This hypothesis was referred to as the humoral theory of the body's defensive system.

The humoral theory was first introduced to the scientific community by George Henry Falkiner Nuttall (1862–1937). His work was greatly influenced by Emil von Behring, who stated, in 1890, that the body's immunity to diseases such as diphtheria and tetanus is dependent upon the capacity of the blood to inactivate the diphtheria or tetanus exotoxin (bacterial poison).

Nuttall worked in 1888 as an assistant at Professor

51

Carl Flugge's Institute of Hygiene, in Göttingen, Germany. Nuttall demonstrated that the defensive and protective substances for immunity were a chemical of the cells present in the blood serum and body fluids. He also demonstrated, through experiments performed *in vitro* (in a test tube), that the protective qualities of the blood were not lost after prolonged standing or heating.

Another researcher, Richard Friedrich Johann Pfeiffer (1858–1945), demonstrated that blood serum destroyed pathogens. Working at the Koch Institute, in Berlin, he developed what is referred to as Pfeiffer's phenomenon and law. Basically, these state that, if an animal is immunized with an attenuated bacteria and then exposed to that same bacteria, the pathogenic form is destroyed. These destroyed bacteria then go through phagocytosis.

Pfeiffer published his findings in 1894, receiving much acclaim for his work. His conclusions were said by some to be as important as those of von Behring and Pasteur.

After Pfeiffer's discoveries, the schism still continued between proponents of the phagocytic and humoral theories. A chief supporter of the humoral theory, and one of the most historically brilliant individuals in the field of immunology, was Paul Ehrlich.

PAUL EHRLICH

Paul Ehrlich, a person who made unique contributions to the field of immunology, was born in 1854 to very well-to-do parents. The family were innkeepers in Upper Silesia, Germany. Ehrlich was the only son in a family of many daughters and, because of this, was spoiled by his parents. His aggressive but pleasant nature brought favorable responses from his parents and the house servants, who went out of their way to please the young child. It was this indulgence in his early years that helped provide a favorable environment for the development of the young boy's curiosity and genius.

Like Pasteur and Metchnikoff, Ehrlich's brilliance was demonstrated in his early school years. He had a great capacity for learning, but was very selective. If he liked a subject, he performed magnificently, but if he did not like a subject, he did miserably. So it was with German composition.

Ehrlich hated writing in German and performed terribly. He loved Latin and did very well. Following this pattern, his love of the sciences brought him excellent grades and a recommendation for further learning. After he finished at the gymnasium (secondary school), Ehrlich decided to study medicine.

Ehrlich began his medical studies at Breslau, but, as was the pattern of the times, attended several universities before finally graduating from the University of Leipzig. While attending universities, his areas of interest were histology (the microscopic study of cells) and the process of staining specimen slides. Staining is very important in studying microscopic specimens. If one is to observe a microscopic organism and see anything of significance, it must be properly stained.

Paul Ehrlich was noted for the originality of his work. Upon graduation from the university, this cigar-smoking, moody, and disheveled genius took up his medical practice at Charité Hospital, Berlin. It was here

German bacteriologist Paul Ehrlich working in his laboratory. He is considered the "father of chemotherapy."

that he put his university studies into practice and developed the technique for staining the tubercular bacillus. His method is still in use today.

In 1886, Ehrlich contracted tuberculosis. He left Charité Hospital and went to Egypt, where he spent two years recuperating in the arid climate. When he recovered, he returned to Berlin to work at the Institute for Infectious Disease, where he began his work in the field of immunology.

During the next six years, 1890–1896, Ehrlich worked with the vegetable poisons ricin and abrin. He demonstrated that animals could be made immune to the poisons through inoculation. He also demonstrated, by using abrin, that a female mammal (including humans), through her milk, passes immunity to specific substances on to her offspring. This is called *passive acquired immunity*. Its effects, however, are short-term, protecting the newborn for only a brief period until the individual develops its own immune capability.

FATHER OF CHEMOTHERAPY

In 1896, Ehrlich began to work on diphtheria antitoxin. He was now director of the Prussian Ministry of Education and Medical Affairs for the Investigation and Control of Sera. It was here that Ehrlich experimented with drugs as agents to kill or stem the growth of pathogens. This is called *chemotherapy*.

For his contributions to the field, Ehrlich is often referred to as the father of chemotherapy. His work in chemotherapy led him to the discovery of treatments for many diseases, such as diphtheria and malaria. At the time of these studies, Ehrlich viewed chemotherapy as a possible panacea for human disease.

In 1900, Ehrlich began to develop his theories on immunity based on antibody production. His views placed him among the humoralists, those who believed that the body's main protection against disease was in the blood serum.

Ehrlich postulated that the blood's antibodies produced side chains that would grow in response to a specific pathogen. These side chains would then attack the pathogen and render it inactive. This theory was called the *side chain theory*. Although the theory has since been discredited, it had a great effect on the medical community at the time, and continued to influence research in immunology for years after Ehrlich's death.

Paul Ehrlich had one of the world's finest scientific minds. His original theories helped to clear the way for future research, and his work served as a unifying force in the field of immunology and chemotherapy. He died on August 20, 1915.

5

A BURST OF KNOWLEDGE AND PRACTICE: 1890–1915

With the twentieth century just ten years away, the science of immunology had become an accepted discipline among the medical professions throughout the world. The germ theory was well in place, and *epidemiology,* the science that analyzes the distributions in human populations of disease and the like, was growing.

Up to this time, the concept of immunity and understanding of the immune response had been developing. Antibodies were discovered and defined, as were antigens. It was now understood that an immune response could be elicited even by nontoxic agents.

Now was the time for further understanding, a time to delve into the subtleties of the immune response, a time to broaden the base of knowledge which would then be used for the ultimate victory against disease.

SEROTHERAPY

Due to Ehrlich's research and the work by von Behring and Kitasato, antibody processes were well known to the scientific community. These researchers and many others had discovered that antibodies were able to:

Neutralize toxins (pathogens);

Clump bacteria, rendering them harmless;

Kill and dissolve bacteria in the presence of normal serum;

Prepare the bacteria for ingestion (phagocytosis);

Sensitize the body for allergic reactions.

These researchers also demonstrated that antibodies are very specific, that is, they act against only one kind of pathogen (for example, tetanus pathogens stimulate antibodies for tetanus, and measles pathogens stimulate antibodies for measles). It was proven that antibodies that fight one kind of pathogen are not effective against others.

Serotherapy led to still more research into antibody properties. Scientists who were working with antibodies now asked: What are they? What can they do?

WHAT ARE
ANTIBODIES?

Michael C. Heidelberger, while studying pneumonia at the Rockefeller Institute, in New York, discovered some fascinating properties of antibodies. He published these findings in a paper entitled "The Soluble Specific Substance of Pneumococcus." This paper revealed that the antibody properties of antisera (serum from an immune animal containing antibodies, immune serum) are attributable to specific protein molecules. These proteins that have antibody activity are called *immunoglobulins*.

Immunoglobulins are found in the blood plasma (serum), and in other tissues and fluids of a person whose immune system is reacting to an outside stimulus. Immunoglobulins are also called Ig molecules.

WHAT CAN
ANTIBODIES DO?

At the time in which research was being conducted into immunoglobulins, Waldemar Mordecai Wolff Haffkine (1860–1930) worked on vaccination against bacterial infections. Haffkine was born in a poor community in Russia, the son of a Jewish schoolmaster. The intellectual atmosphere in which he was raised helped to steer him toward the study of science at the University of Odessa, where he was greatly influenced by Metchnikoff, who supervised his studies.

59

After graduation, Haffkine worked in Russia for five years, until oppression against Jews caused him to emigrate to Switzerland, where he worked for a year. He then went to the Pasteur Institute, in Paris, where, once again, he joined with his mentor, Metchnikoff.

In 1891, Haffkine began his researches into protective immunization against the disease cholera. Using Pasteur's method of experimentation, he worked with laboratory animals. Testing one animal, he found that vaccination with a weakened strain of the pathogen would cause a severe local reaction and a fever, but would do no other harm. Taking his research one step further, six days later he vaccinated the same animal with a virulent strain, which also produced no harm.

Haffkine tested his vaccination theory on himself and survived. He then experimented with the process on

Six-year-old Randy Kerr receives the first Salk polio vaccine, a killed vaccine, in April of 1954. As the result of vaccinations, the number of cases of paralytic poliomyelitis in the United States dropped from an annual rate of twenty-one thousand to just seven cases in 1974. Another vaccine used was a live-attenuated virus, known as the Sabin-type vaccine.

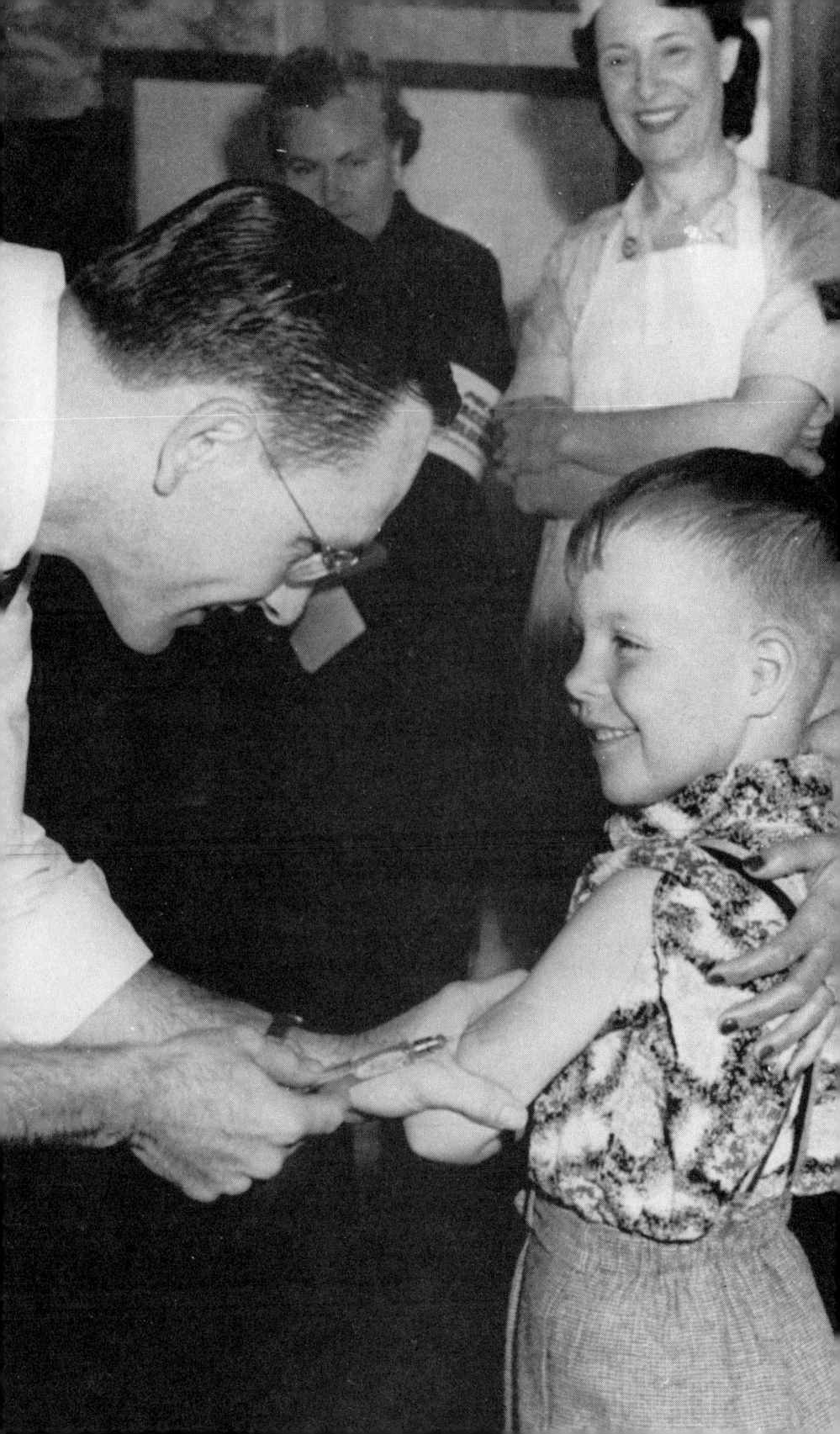

three volunteers, who were friends of his. They also survived. He assumed his immunization method was safe.

Haffkine left Europe for India, where he worked on his cholera-vaccination theories, with much success. During this time, the pathogen that caused bubonic plague was isolated by Kitasato. Haffkine, upon hearing of Kitasato's discovery, left his work with cholera and went to work in developing a vaccine against the plague.

In India, Haffkine first tried his plague vaccine on prisoners in a Bombay jail. The results of his experiments were highly successful. The prisoners were protected by Haffkine's *killed vaccine*. A killed vaccine is a preparation derived from a killed pathogen, which is still strong enough to supply antigens which will induce *active acquired immunity*. Active acquired immunity occurs when the body develops immunity as a result of exposure to a specific antigen and then produces antibodies against that antigen.

Haffkine's killed vaccines caused the body to produce antibodies. Thus, when the fatal dose of live pathogen came, the body's memory was quick to produce even more antibodies, which prevented the disease from taking hold.

Haffkine was the first person to apply prophylactic (protective) immunization to people. Further work in this area was done by other researchers.

VACCINE THERAPY

Almroth Edward Wright (1861–1947) initiated the era of vaccine therapy. He was the son of a clergyman, grew up in Ireland, and later received scholarships to study medicine at the University of Leipzig, in Germany. He became interested in the science of immunology through the influence of his friend Wooldridge.

Following an 1893 meeting and consultation with Haffkine, Wright began experimenting with the typhoid bacillus, which causes typhus. Wright heat-killed these bacilli before injecting them into people. As a precaution, these first injections were not for immunization purposes but to test for local reaction to the drug.

After reading a paper on killed vaccines by Richard F. J. Pfeiffer, Wright was convinced that killed vaccines could produce immunity to disease. To test his theory, he began to inoculate people with heat-killed typhoid bacilli. The results of these vaccinations convinced him that this type of vaccination did produce some immunity to the disease.

In 1898, while experimenting with brucellosis (commonly known as undulant fever), Wright decided that the best way to test his theories would be to inoculate himself. He became seriously ill, suffering throughout the rest of that year.

Wright's bout with brucellosis did not deter his determination, however. He continued his work with typhoid and eventually reached the conclusion that small doses of the vaccine did not produce a negative effect and did provide immunity. With Wright's publication of a paper on his experimentations, the era of vaccine therapy had arrived.

Wright was also involved in research which eventually ended the phagocytic-humoral controversy. In 1903, while working with Stewart Douglass, another physician, Wright came to the conclusion that neither the phagocytic nor humoral theories was totally correct or wrong. He postulated that they both were correct. This revelation came to Wright as he and Douglass discovered *opsonins,* substances which aid the process of phagocytosis. This discovery eliminated the differences between the cellularists and the humoralists.

IMMUNOCHEMISTRY

Immunochemistry is the study of the chemical factors affecting immunity. The term "immunochemistry" was first used in the decade after 1900, as scientists published their theories emphasizing the importance of chemistry in immunology.

The first major contribution of immunochemistry to immunology was the study of haptens, by Karl Landsteiner (1868–1943). A *hapten* is a chemical that is capable of combining with an antibody molecule, and incapable of stimulating an immune response unless it is chemically united with an antigen as a carrier. He demonstrated that these chemicals could be attached to already existing antigens. This binding would change the specificity of the antigen, proving very helpful in understanding molecular mechanisms of immune response.

Landsteiner was born in Vienna, Austria. He studied medicine and chemistry with his mentor, Emil Fisher. At the Pathology Institute, in Vienna, he studied the agglutinative (clumping) properties of human blood. He found that when one person's blood is mixed with another's, it will clump. He also noticed that blood samples have different patterns of clumping when mixed with control samples. He labeled qualities resulting in these patterns A, B, and O blood groups. His researches further led him to discover that blood samples of the same group will not clump when mixed. This discovery made possible the use of blood transfusions.

Landsteiner later moved to the United States, where he carried on research at the Rockefeller Institute, in New York. Here he discovered the Rh factor (rhesus factor) in blood.

For his work with human blood, Landsteiner was awarded the Nobel Prize for Medicine in 1930. His brilliant career ended with his death in 1943.

6

VIRUSES AND VACCINES

The immunological research of the latter part of the nineteenth century was devoted mainly to bacterial diseases. It was not until the 1930s that a breakthrough occurred that bent the science of immunology to examine viruses.

Viruses, unlike bacteria, will not grow in a medium (artificial culture). They will grow only in living cells (live tissue cultures or organisms). It was the discovery of how to grow live viruses that broadened the horizons of the science of immunology.

The term "virus" has been in use for centuries. It comes from the Latin meaning "poison," but by the eighteenth century had come to mean a poisonous substance in the body, especially one capable of being transferred from one living thing to another. Louis Pasteur made no distinction between "virus" and "bacteria." He used the term "virus" to describe the causative agents of cholera and rabies. Cholera, in fact, is caused by a bacterium, rabies by a virus.

SMALLER THAN BACTERIA

Friedrich Löffler (1852–1915), a German bacteriologist working with Koch in 1898, discovered a transmissible animal disease in which a virus seemed to be the causative agent. They were working with foot-and-mouth disease when they found that the causative agent could pass through a bacteriological filter, a filter that stops bacteria from passing through. Hence they called it a filterable virus. In order to pass through a filter fine enough to stop a microscopic bacterium, the filterable virus had to be even more minute.

In 1898, Martinus Beijerinck, a Dutch bacteriologist from Delft, also described a filterable virus, this time as the cause of tobacco-mosaic disease, a disease affecting the leaves of tobacco plants and easily spread from one plant to another. Beijerinck described the qualities of the filterable virus and, for his time, was the first to have a good understanding of the organism.

Some of the qualities Beijerinck attributed to the virus still apply today:

A virus can multiply only in living cells.

A virus can remain dormant without losing its infectious qualities.

A virus can be inactivated by boiling.

From his researches, Beijerinck postulated that there were many diseases in both plants and animals that were most likely caused by viruses and transmitted, in many instances, by vectors. A *vector* is an organism that carries pathogens from one host to another.

Walter Reed (1851–1902), a Virginia-born surgeon and bacteriologist, theorized that yellow fever was caused by a virus that was transmitted by an insect vector, the mosquito. To prove his hypothesis, in 1900, Reed set up a special army camp in Cuba where volunteers were exposed to mosquitoes. His hypothesis was proven correct when those volunteers, after being bitten, came down with the disease.

In 1915, Frederick Twort (1877–1950), a London physician, was the first to discover a new class of viruses called *bacteriophages,* viruses that affect bacteria, not plant or animal cells.

In 1917, Felix d'Herelle, a French Canadian educated in Paris and Montreal, carried Twort's discovery further. While working at the Pasteur Institute, d'Herelle demonstrated that bacteria contaminated with a virus can serve as vectors for transmission of the virus.

GROWING VIRUSES

As early as 1911, S. M. Copeman had published an article in which he described a method of using fertile chicken eggs to cultivate a virus for developing a vaccine. Copeman's method, although sound, was not widely accepted at the time.

In the mid-1920s, other scientists began research with growing live viruses. In 1925, the team of Parker and Nye was successful in growing herpes simplex virus on the tissue of the testicles of rabbits, which tissue was then explanted (removed) from the testicle into a test tube.

These first experiments in cultivation required great skill, persistence, and creativity by the researcher. Knowledge was limited, and many postulates were erroneous. For example, at this time, many believed that viruses could grow only on cells that were actively dividing. This hypothesis was later disproved by H. B. Maitland, a microbiologist.

Maitland demonstrated, by growing a virus on hen kidneys, that it was possible to cultivate a virus on cells that are not dividing. His method was not further developed, however.

In 1931, a breakthrough occurred in virology. Ernest William Goodpasture (1886–1960)—working at Vanderbilt University, in Nashville, Tennessee—developed systematic methods for using a fertilized chicken egg to cultivate viruses. His research served as the prototype for developing the use of the chick embryo as a medium for growing viruses.

Research in virology continued, with many experimenters now using Goodpasture's methods. However, the scientists' research was hampered. Although they knew what a virus was and how it grew and behaved, no one had yet seen one. It was not until the late 1930s that the electron microscope was developed. This was to be the tool which would open up a new era in the study of viruses.

With the development of electronics and the vacuum tube, the eventual invention of the electron microscope became inevitable. In 1939, several German scientists reported observing tobacco-mosaic virus under their electron microscope.

In 1941, in the United States, Ladislaus Laszio Marton, working at RCA, introduced the practical use of the electron microscope in the medical professions. This device furthered the science of virology by exposing viruses to much closer study.

The development of antibiotics such as penicillin and streptomycin made it possible to keep viral cultures free from bacterial contamination. An antibiotic will destroy bacteria, but not viruses. Pure cultures enabled the quality and type of viral cultivation to improve.

The next step forward in the field of virology came with the development of tissue-culture techniques. This led to the improved ability to cultivate viruses in the laboratory and develop methods of prevention and/or treatment.

In 1949, research bacteriologist John Franklin Enders demonstrated that poliomyelitis viruses could be grown on cells from monkey kidneys. He isolated and typed three strains of polio virus. His work made possible the future development of a "killed" polio-virus vaccine by Jonas Salk. For his work, Enders was awarded the 1954 Nobel Prize for Medicine. It was Enders and his colleagues who set the stage for modern methods for producing vaccines to combat viruses. Enders himself helped develop a typhus vaccine. He also isolated the measles virus and then developed a "live" measles-virus vaccine.

The research goes on today in the continuing battle against viruses. Due to modern technology, isolation of new strains takes very little time. Once the virus is identified, the search begins for a method of disarming the pathogen, using one of three approaches: developing (1) a "killed" or (2) a "live" vaccine that will immunize people against the virus, or (3) the use of chemotherapy, which involves the identification or development of drugs that will selectively destroy the reproductive capability of the virus.

The future provides a new challenge to researchers in the field of virology. The AIDS virus, HIV (human immunodeficiency virus), may be the most serious infectious challenge to human mortality since the bubonic plague. Thus far, medical science is baffled by this deadly disease, but the research goes on and, eventually, a way for combating this pernicious virus will be discovered. (See Chapter 8 for more on the AIDS virus.)

7

ANTIBODY THEORIES

Modern immunological science has now progressed to some understanding of the chemical nature of antibodies and antigens, and the potential for developing better immunogens (vaccines, etc.). This, along with increased knowledge of the genetic makeup of cells, has put the science of immunology on the forefront of new perspectives for fighting disease.

Researchers in immunology now know the following about the immune system.

An antibody is a *protein* molecule produced in response to stimulation by an antigen, and is capable of combining specifically with that antigen. An antibody possesses two distinct properties: *specificity,* the ability to bind only to certain antigens; and *effector function,* the ability then to interact with inflammatory cells and certain soluble serum molecules to cause either the removal of the antigen or the destruction of the organism that carries the antigen.

Antigens are molecules which, when introduced into an organism, are able to stimulate the production of antibodies capable of interacting with them. These antigens, sometimes called immunogens, are the trigger for the immune response.

The *immune response* is the body's ability to distinguish between self and nonself. *Self* refers to the body's own antigens, and *nonself* to the antigens of foreign invaders. When foreign antigens enter the body, specialized cells of the immune system respond.

Lymphocytes are white blood cells whose function is to identify and destroy nonself antigens. Lymphocytes originate in the reticuloendothelial system, which includes cells of the liver, thymus, spleen, lymph nodes, and bone marrow. There are two general types of lymphocytes, *B cells* and *T cells*.

It is believed that B cells mature in the bone marrow, where they develop *receptors,* which enable them to recognize and react with antigens. Just as specific keys fit specific locks, each receptor is unique to the specific qualities of an antigen. When an organism is invaded, the B cells attack. As the B cell comes in contact with the antigen it is designed to combine with, a series of events takes place.

The B cell divides into a colony of *plasma cells,* each one an exact copy, or *clone,* of the activated B cell. These B cells instantly manufacture antibodies, which combat the specific antigen in several ways. The antibody may match the shape of the antigen and attach itself to the antigen, thus rendering the antigen harmless. The antibody may also attach to more than one antigen and cause agglutination (clumping), again rendering the antigen harmless.

This theory on antibody production is called the clonal selection theory, for which Macfarlane Burnet won the 1960 Nobel Prize for Medicine. The theory states that lymphocytes have antigen receptors and commit an antibody to combine with a specific antigen. When this occurs, the B cells divide and produce daughter cells with the same specificity as the original cell. The theory explains the ongoing increase in antibody attraction to antigens over time. In other words, a weak dose of an antigen starts the process. Then, when a stronger, perhaps fatal, dose is introduced, the antibodies respond and protect the organism.

T cells are lymphocytes which travel through the blood to the thymus gland, in the chest, where they mature. Some T cells help to regulate antibody production of B cells. Helper T cells increase antibody production while suppressor T cells reduce it. Killer T cells may also destroy antigens by directly killing bacteria, viruses, and even some of the person's own cells that have mutated to become cancer cells.

The T cells and B cells actively compete for a limited amount of foreign antigen. Those cells that form the strongest bonds with antigen are selectively stimulated to divide to produce many similar progeny. This is what Burnet referred to when stating that there is an ongoing increase in antibody attraction to antigens over time. Both

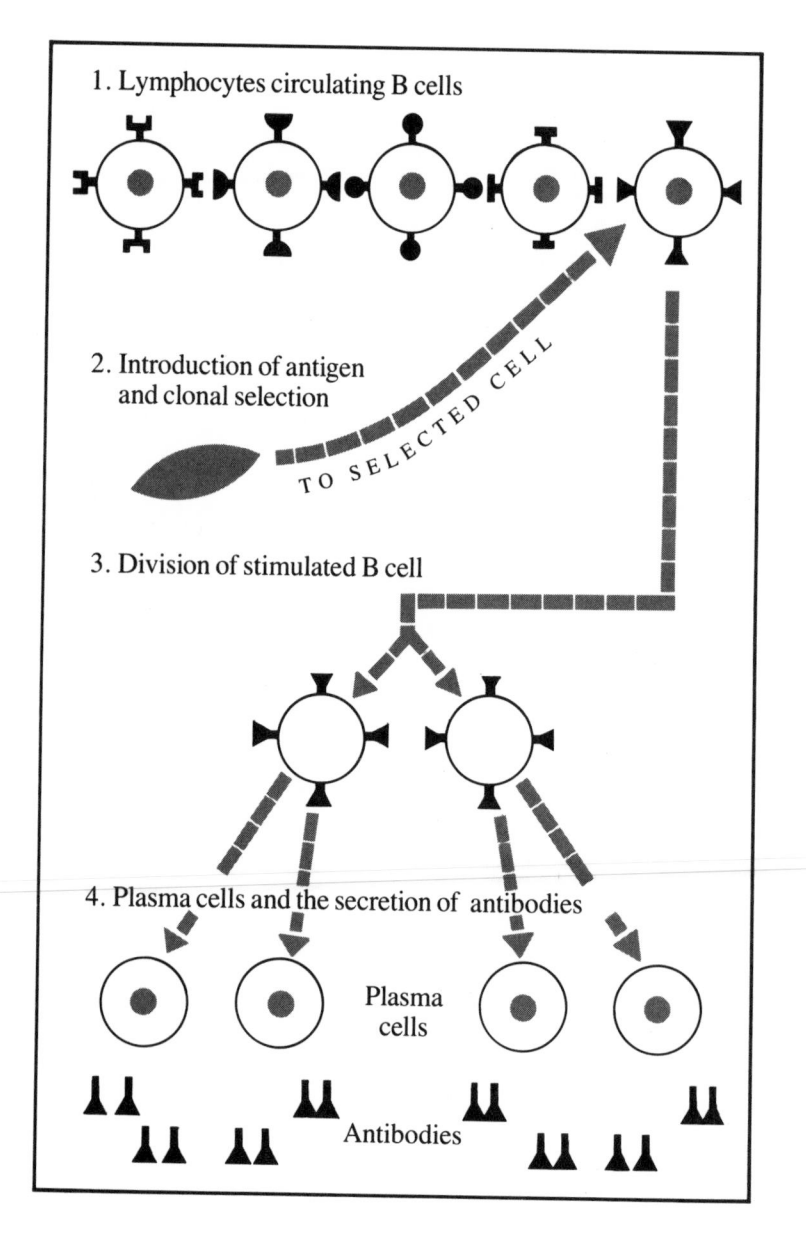

1. Lymphocytes circulating B cells

2. Introduction of antigen and clonal selection

TO SELECTED CELL

3. Division of stimulated B cell

4. Plasma cells and the secretion of antibodies

Plasma cells

Antibodies

Clonal Selection Theory

T cells and B cells produce memory cells that remain in the body for years.

A response to a repeat attack is called active acquired immunity because the body has developed immunity as the result of the primary exposure to a specific antigen. The secondary response is swift, and many antibodies are produced to combine with the foreign antigen.

MONOCLONAL ANTIBODIES

Antibody theory in the 1980s has advanced very rapidly through the use of modern technology. The possibilities for answers in combating disease have grown exponentially, as researchers take advantage of the computer, the electron microscope, and *genetic engineering*.

Biotechnology is a new field of biology in which technology is helping to develop biologic drugs and diagnostic reagents. A *biologic* is any substance derived from a living organism. One method for making biologics is the production and use of *monoclonal antibodies*. The method for producing monoclonal antibodies was discovered by Georges Köhler and César Milstein. They created monoclonal antibodies to produce an inexhaustible source of highly specific antibodies.

Monoclonal antibodies are created by fusing antibody-forming cells with malignant (cancerous) plasma cells. This fusion produces a hybrid cell, referred to as a *hybridoma*.

The malignant cell genes contribute to the hybri-

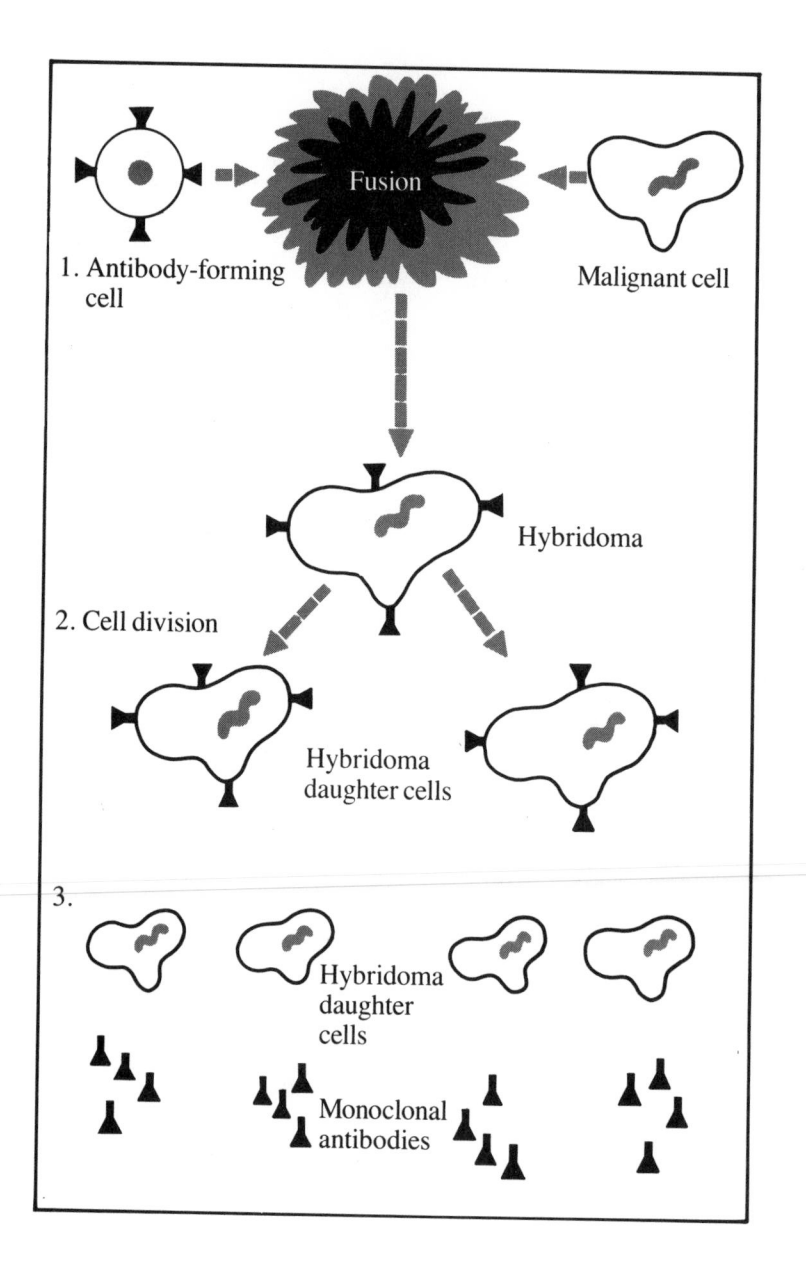

1. Antibody-forming cell

Fusion

Malignant cell

Hybridoma

2. Cell division

Hybridoma daughter cells

3.

Hybridoma daughter cells

Monoclonal antibodies

Production of Monoclonal Antibodies

doma cell their tendency to unchecked cell reproduction, while the B-cell genes contribute the ability to produce a specific antibody. All of the progeny cells, called a "clone" of the original hybridoma cell, retain these properties. The antibodies produced are called monoclonal antibodies because they all come from the clone of a single fused cell. A population of monoclonal-antibody molecules is much more homogeneous than a population of polyclonal antibody molecules obtained from an animal (including human beings).

The full usefulness of monoclonal antibodies is yet to be discovered, but immunologists today use them in new techniques as in-vitro diagnostic tools for immunological studies. Monoclonal antibodies have also been used in vivo to deliver radioactivity specifically to tumors for locating and imaging the cancer, and to deliver toxic drugs to tumors in order to provide direct chemotherapy.

NEW FRONTIERS IN IMMUNOLOGY

Some scientists predict that within the next ten years we will be seeing new vaccines to prevent diseases that are, up to this time, incurable. Perhaps there will be a single vaccine to give permanent protection against a number of pathogens. The possibilities are endless, and the potential for benefits to human life enormous. How will all this come about?

Through the science of genetic engineering, researchers are working with DNA *(deoxyribonucleic acid)*, which is found in every cell of every living thing. Every cell of the human body has forty-six *chromosomes* (tiny strands of DNA) covered with thousands of *genes* (concentrations of DNA). The chromosomes and genes contain the blueprint for the individual person. Everything that a person is genetically is determined by the DNA, the chemical material that controls inherited information. Among this information is susceptibility to disease.

In the past, vaccines were made from attenuated strains of any given pathogen. These weakened forms of the disease would excite the immune system and stimulate antibody production. Some of these antibodies, after the threat to the individual was gone, would remain circulating in the bloodstream, giving the individual immunity to the disease.

Today, Enzo Paoletti, a genetic researcher, using genetic engineering, is making a new kind of vaccine. Using Jenner's smallpox vaccine, because the virus is relatively large, Paoletti uses a *gene-splicing* technique to make a new vaccine. Foreign genes are spliced into the cowpox virus, and the *vaccinia* (cowpox virus) is fooled into producing this foreign antigen. For example, if the influenza virus is spliced into vaccinia, vaccinia will be tricked into producing the influenza antigen.

Not only are Paoletti's genetically engineered vaccines less expensive and easier to produce than traditional vaccines, but there is also less risk of the vaccine causing the disease, because only a few genes are required to stimulate the immune response. Eventually, Paoletti hopes to be able to develop a genetically engineered vaccine that will provide multiple immunity with one inoculation.

GENE THERAPY

Genetic engineering is also being used to fight certain fatal diseases. Through the method of gene splicing, scientists alter the material of life, DNA. This is called gene therapy, and the tool is a virus. Scientists are experimenting with viruses by stripping them of their pathogenic genes. The virus is no longer a threat to the host organism but, if artificially injected into a cell, can still infect that cell.

In this manner, researchers, after disarming the virus, splice into the viral chromosomes the desired human genes. The modified virus is then injected into the body, delivering the spliced genes into the host cell. It is hoped that these artificially inserted genes will be able to offset the inherited mistake caused by a genetic disease.

Here is how the process of gene therapy works:

Researchers isolate a virus from an animal.

The virus is then rendered harmless by stripping it of its genes for reproduction. What remains is a modified virus still capable of combining with a human host cell, becoming part of the host DNA.

A human gene is spliced into the modified virus.

Some of the diseased human cells are extracted from an individual and incubated in a dish with the genetically engineered virus. At this time, the recombinant virus enters the diseased cells and becomes part of the DNA.

The treated cells are now returned to the individual, where the correction will produce enough functional gene product to offset and perhaps even to cure the disease.

Gene therapy is now in its initial stages, with testing restricted to laboratory animals. It is an approach whose usefulness is yet to be proven by human experimentation. But, if gene therapy works, the benefits would be astounding. Diseases such as Tay-Sachs disease, which causes blindness or mental retardation; hemophilia, a bleeding disease; and many others would be able to be cured.

IMMUNOTHERAPY

Another biotechnology method being studied today specifically to fight cancer is immunotherapy. Cancer is a pernicious disease which every year takes the lives of over half a million Americans. At the National Cancer Institute (NCI), in Bethesda, Maryland, research is being done with drugs that will help an individual's own immune system to fight cancer. This treatment is called adoptive immunotherapy. This is a more accurate and aggressive form of chemotherapy. Using a biologic drug called interleukin-2 (IL-2), the activity of the body's own lymphocytes (white blood cells) is enhanced. This occurs when the lymphocytes are cultured in a test tube with the IL-2.

Here is how the IL-2 process works:

Millions of lymphocytes are removed from an individual.

These lymphocytes are cultured with the drug IL-2.

After seventy-two hours, the lymphocytes are transformed to lymphokine-activated killer (LAK) cells.

These LAK cells, plus more IL-2, are put back into the individual's body to attack the cancer.

So far, experimental results have been promising, but there are bad side effects from the drug. It will take much more research before this drug can be widely used.

Monoclonal antibodies are also being used in the battle against cancer. Lymphocytes from an individual are incubated with specific monoclonal antibodies. These monoclonal antibodies are directed against a specific cancer. After incubation, the mixture is injected back into the individual. The antibody-treated lymphocytes travel directly to the cancer, where they can have a maximum effect in fighting the disease.

Many other methods of immunotherapy are being studied today, as scientists the world over ally themselves to fight cancer. *Gamma interferon,* a biologic chemical produced by T cells, now is being synthesized in laboratories. When injected into individuals, this drug seems to make some cancers more susceptible to the immune system. Tumor necrosis factor is a tumor-killing chemical manufactured by the white blood cells, and which is now being tested for use in people. Colony-stimulating factors are chemicals that work together to stimulate *macrophages,* scavenger cells of the immune system. The hope is that the macrophages will kill cancer cells.

All of the new techniques and treatments described in this chapter are highly experimental. None have, as yet, been adopted as approved standard treatments for disease. Although scientists are hopeful, there are many problems of safety and effectiveness yet to be overcome. Many treatments have side effects that may be worse for the patient than the disease itself. Some of these side effects are loss of hair, loss of appetite, vomiting, diarrhea, Bell's palsy, a combination of any of these, and possibly death.

As for genetic engineering, there are inherent dangers that must be recognized. Some scientists fear that these experiments will create new mutant organisms that will cause worse problems than before. Others fear the new genetic technology could be used for malevolent purposes. Finally, there are some who think it is ethically wrong to fool with the natural order of things.

8

AIDS AND OTHER DISORDERS OF THE IMMUNE SYSTEM

When a person's immune system does not function properly, a host of disorders may develop. These disorders can be put into three categories: allergies, autoimmune diseases, and immune-deficiency diseases.

A properly functioning immune system easily recognizes foreign antigens, producing antibodies to render them harmless and only attacking the foreign cells. It is when a person's immune system does not make the distinction between self and nonself and attacks the body's own cells that problems occur.

T cells play a major role as chemical mediators in activating the immune response. Antibodies produced by B cells that have been activated by the T cells belong to the immunoglobulin family of proteins, of which there are five major types: G, A, M, E, and D. Each of these individual classes of immunoglobulin functions in a different role. IgG antibodies protect people from infection and allergic people from attacks. Both IgG and IgM activate the complement system of blood enzymes involved in the immune response.

In 1966, Drs. Kimishige Ishizaka and Teruko Ishizaka, while working at the Children's Asthma Research Institute and Hospital in Denver, Colorado, discovered that it is the IgE antibody that is responsible for the majority of allergic reactions. They and other researchers have found that people who suffer from allergies have as much as ten times the IgE in their blood as nonallergic people.

FIGHTING
ALLERGIES

Antigens that cause allergies are called *allergens*. An *allergy* is an extreme sensitivity to a specific antigen. Allergens cause the immune system to produce IgE antibodies, which attach themselves to *mast cells*. Mast cells are usually found in the respiratory system, gastrointestinal tract, and the skin.

IgE antibodies also attach to *basophils*, a type of white blood cell. Basophils are found circulating in the bloodstream. As many as half a million IgE molecules may attach to a single basophil.

The IgE antibodies cause these cells to release potent chemicals, such as *histamines,* which produce many of the familiar allergic symptoms. The effect on the body often depends on the type of antigen and method of entry. Inhaled allergens, such as pollen or dust, usually cause respiratory problems, i.e., runny nose, itchy and swollen eyes, and/or constriction of the bronchial tubes. Antigens ingested in food may cause hives, rashes, sometimes vomiting, and often diarrhea.

Histamines dilate blood vessels, which causes seepage of fluids. They also constrict the bronchial tubes, causing swelling and, consequently, difficulty in breathing.

The most common treatment for allergic reaction is with an antihistamine drug. As implied by its name, an antihistamine fights the effects of histamine. More serious forms of allergies, such as asthma, must be controlled with stronger drugs under strict medical supervision. The drugs used in treatment of these allergies include *steroids,* a class of hormones used to reduce swelling.

Dr. Ray Patterson, chief of medicine and head of the allergy section at Northwestern University Medical School in Evanston, Illinois, has developed a new series of allergy shots which, with one-quarter of the standard number of injections, produces immunity.

At the Medical Biology Institute in La Jolla, California, studies being done with mice indicate that there may be a type of "on-off switch" that controls allergic reactions. The suspected switch is a substance called SFA, or suppressive factor of allergy. SFA is produced by the lymphocytes and prevents the production of IgE.

Dr. Lawrence Lichtenstein, of the Johns Hopkins Medical School in Baltimore, in another study, has revealed that *arachidonic acid* is a major component of allergic reactions. He believes that this discovery will lead to the development of more-potent and more-effective medications for treatment of allergies.

WARRING FACTIONS OF THE IMMUNE SYSTEM

Autoimmune means immunity to oneself. Autoimmune disease occurs when the body's own antibodies act against its own antigens. There are many types of autoimmune diseases, with many of these diseases specific to a single bodily organ or gland. Autoimmune hemolytic anemia (AHA) is an autoimmune disease in which the body makes antibodies against its own red blood cells.

There are very few body organs that are not affected by autoimmune disease if the disease chooses to attack. Autoimmune diseases can specifically attack the heart, lungs, kidneys, liver, muscles, endocrine glands, and the skin. Multiple sclerosis, a disease that destroys a brain tissue called myelin, is an autoimmune disease.

Some autoimmune diseases may attack more than a single body organ or gland. This type of immune dysfunction is referred to as a *systemic* (affecting the body as a whole) autoimmune disease. Lupus, a systemic autoimmune disease, attacks the kidneys, vascular system, skin, and joints.

Autoimmune diseases are treated with drugs called *immunosuppressants*. As the name indicates, this type of drug suppresses the immune response. Immunosuppressants are also used to treat patients who have received a donor organ. These drugs prevent the recipient's body from rejecting the transplanted organ.

There are some inherent difficulties with immunosuppressant drugs. One of the main problems is that, because these drugs suppress the immune system, they reduce the body's ability to fight infectious disease.

DEFENSELESS BODIES

The opposite of an autoimmune disease is an *immune deficiency disease*. An immune deficiency disease occurs when a person's immune system is not doing what it is supposed to do, i.e., protect the body against disease.

Severe combined immunodeficiency (SCID) is a severe form of immunodeficiency disease. Through a birth defect or genetic malfunction, a child may be born without enough B cells and T cells to defend himself or herself. This renders the child susceptible to infectious disease. You may have heard of children being raised in protective bubbles. These children have SCID.

Human immunodeficiency virus (HIV) produces the most dangerous of all immunodeficiency diseases—acquired immune deficiency syndrome (AIDS).

AIDS is an infectious disease, whose relentless spread today is threatening a large portion of Earth's population. It is a relatively new disease, which probably originated in Central Africa, possibly as a result of a mutation of a monkey virus which developed into a new strain pathogenic for humans.

Up until 1982, infectious AIDS, as we currently understand it, was unheard of. In fact, research indicates that in 1965 AIDS did not exist.

It is devastating to know that today, in the United States alone, there are over fifty thousand reported cases of AIDS, and another million and a half people who are thought to be infected carriers. If AIDS continues to progress unchecked, the Centers for Disease Control (CDC), in Atlanta, Georgia, predicts the total number of cases in the United States will be over a quarter of a million by 1992.

AIDS is caused by HIV, which is a retrovirus. A *retrovirus* is an RNA-containing virus that reproduces by making DNA from its RNA within the cells it infects. This is the opposite of the usual situation, in which RNA is made from DNA, hence the name "retro," or "reverse," virus. The AIDS virus infects the T cells. After infection, the T cells are destroyed, rendering the victim defenseless against many diseases, which eventually cause death.

THE SPREAD OF AIDS

How can the AIDS virus be transmitted? Researchers have identified the AIDS virus in blood, saliva, semen, tears, and urine. Yet, although the virus has been identified in all these body fluids, the evidence accumulated up to now strongly suggests that the AIDS virus can be

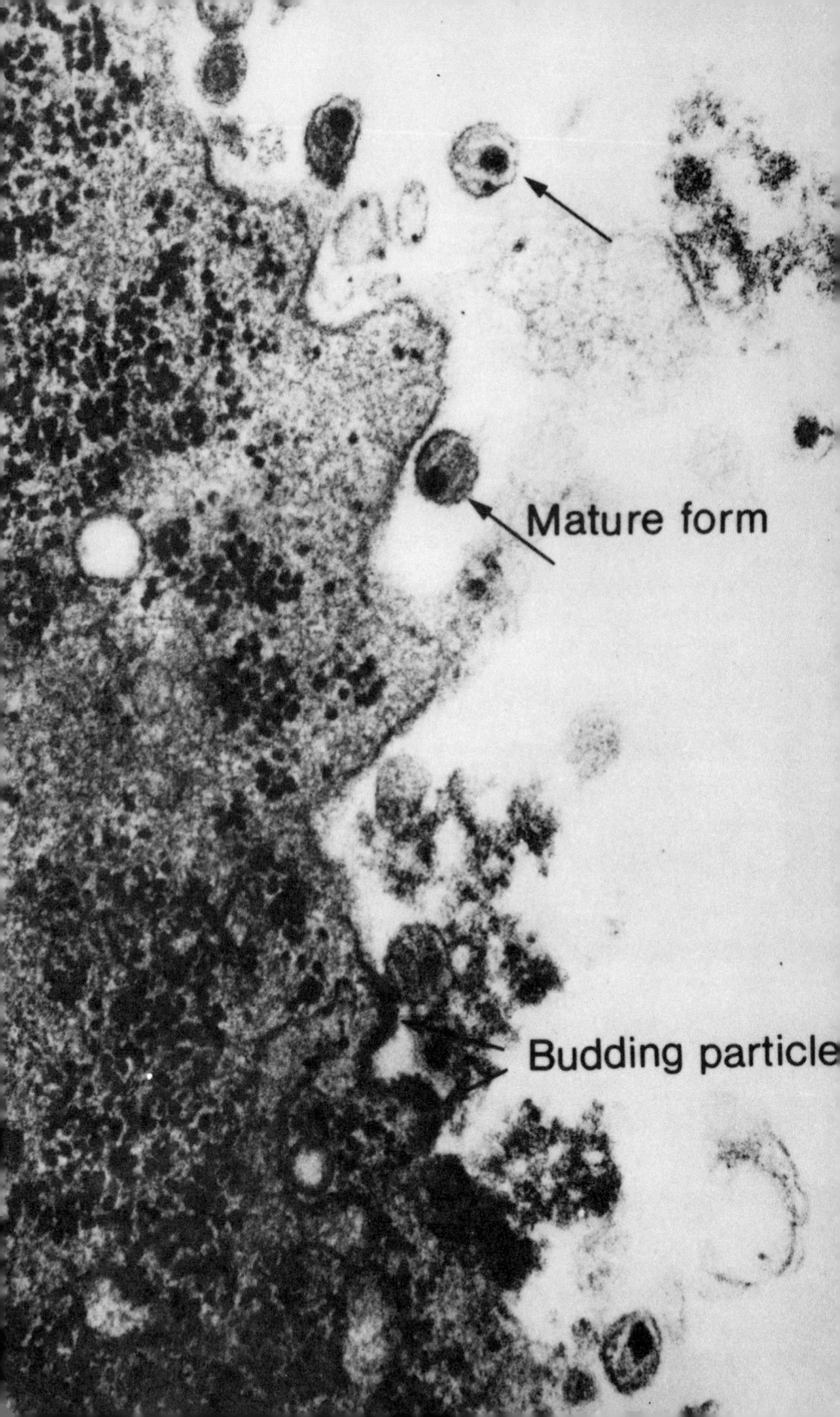

Mature form

Budding particle

transmitted only through intimate sexual contact or through direct entry into the bloodstream. AIDS does not appear to be transmitted through casual contact.

Approximately 70 percent of the AIDS victims in the United States to date are male homosexuals, about 15 percent are drug addicts, and approximately 2 percent have contracted the disease through blood transfusions. Only a very small percentage of AIDS cases seem to have been transmitted heterosexually, and usually from males to females.

AIDS appears to be spreading rapidly. It is uncertain whether all persons exposed to the AIDS virus will come down with the disease. Why some people are more susceptible than others is not yet clear. To date, the statistics show that at least 10 percent of those infected with the AIDS virus will actually come down with the disease. However, this estimate has been revised upward as more follow-up time has elapsed; some researchers believe that in the future this percentage will increase markedly.

There is a test to ascertain whether a person has been exposed to the AIDS virus. The blood test looks for an antibody against the virus. The presence of this antibody means that the person has been exposed to the AIDS virus.

Once identified, the AIDS carriers can take precautionary measures to ensure that other people are not ex-

Highly magnified photograph
of the AIDS virus

posed to the virus through them. The problems with this include the following:

The AIDS tests are not completely reliable. So-called false positives occur, especially in low-risk groups. Confirmatory tests are necessary.

People are hesitant to take the blood test to see if they have been exposed because of fear, especially fear of discrimination if the test is positive.

Once identified, people who have tested positive to the AIDS virus do not always take the precautionary steps necessary to prevent the spread of AIDS.

Carriers do not always register positive when first infected.

In a free society, the movements, rights, and privacy of the individuals who show positive for AIDS cannot, must not, be abridged.

AIDS is thought to be spread through intimate contact, usually sexual, which results in exchange of body fluids like semen or blood. If a person has a sexual encounter with someone who has tested positive for the AIDS virus, there is a chance that he or she has become infected with the virus.

The AIDS virus (HIV) is also spread through blood transfusions. If an HIV carrier has given blood, and this blood is transfused into another person, that person will also become an HIV carrier. Today, blood centers around

Myths about AIDS

Myth 1. AIDS is a homosexual disease. *False.* Although in the United States today most victims of the disease are within the male homosexual community, AIDS is found in heterosexuals as well. AIDS is indiscriminate. It affects both males and females, and adults and children of all races.

Myth 2. AIDS can be spread through casual contact. *False.* Shaking hands, coughing, sneezing, crying, preparing food, hugging, or talking will not transmit the AIDS virus.

Myth 3. AIDS can be gotten from toilets, swimming pools, and hot tubs. *False.* The AIDS virus must be transmitted directly into the blood. AIDS *cannot* be contracted from toilet seats, hot tubs, swimming pools, or bed linens. You cannot get AIDS by sharing household equipment or appliances with a person who has AIDS.

Myth 4. Quarantining carriers will help to prevent the spread of AIDS. *False.* Quarantine is useless with AIDS, because AIDS is not spread by casual contact. People who know they have AIDS should willingly not have intimate (that is, sexual) contact with others.

the nation protect recipients from the AIDS virus by testing all donors. If a donor tests positive for AIDS, then that individual's blood is not used.

Another method of transmission of the AIDS virus is through sharing of unsterilized hypodermic needles. This is common among intravenous drug abusers. Because many drug abusers are heterosexual, if exposed to the virus, they spread it to a person of the opposite sex when they have a sexual encounter.

IMMUNOLOGY'S GREAT CHALLENGE

Currently, major resources have been committed to many top-notch researchers who are diligently seeking a cure for AIDS or a vaccine to prevent its spread. Scientists at Burroughs Wellcome Company of Research Triangle Park, North Carolina, have developed a drug called Retrovir (also called zidovudene, *azidothymidine,* or *AZT*).

One of the myths about AIDS is that it can be transmitted through casual contact. Here a parent assists children with signs protesting a decision made by the city of New York to allow a second-grader with AIDS to attend school.

This drug, although not a cure for the disease, does seem to help ease the symptoms of some of the AIDS victims. But this drug, like many other experimental drugs, has some very dangerous side effects. Retrovir can damage the bone marrow of people who use it, and has also been found to have increased the susceptibility to some diseases in some recipients.

Research is also going on to develop a vaccine that will prevent healthy people from being infected with the AIDS virus. Because the AIDS virus mutates so rapidly, the immune system has difficulty manufacturing antibodies to match the antigens. Thus, the development of a vaccine is difficult at best. By the time a vaccine is developed, the virus has mutated and a new strain, for which a defense has not been manufactured, is ready to take over the attack.

For a vaccine to work, it must stimulate antibodies that will attack and kill the invader while it is in the blood. Because the AIDS virus can move from one T cell to another without returning to the blood, it is also very difficult to manufacture a vaccine against the disease.

The problem of the mutating genes has to be dealt with before an effective vaccine can be found. Presently researchers are looking for a constant among the mutants, an antigen that has remained the same despite the mutations. If this antigen is found, an effective vaccine might be able to be developed.

Another method in the vaccine search is the use of vaccinia, the live smallpox virus. Researchers are attempting to splice a benign piece of the AIDS virus into vaccinia. Thus far, the research, done with monkeys, has been encouraging. But these tests are still in the very early stages, and significant results have yet to come.

Myron Essex, a researcher at Harvard University, in Cambridge, Massachusetts, is experimenting with a method used by Jenner almost three hundred years ago. There is a recently discovered African virus, called HTLV-IV, that very closely resembles the AIDS virus. Essex's theory is that, if people are vaccinated with HTLV-IV, they might be afforded protection against AIDS. Research is now being done with some Africans who are at risk of getting AIDS. Should the results be positive, the AIDS virus could possibly be eliminated.

In Sweden, a new drug, peptide T, is being experimented with as a cure for AIDS. Peptide T acts like the AIDS virus and, when in the body, goes to the AIDS receptors. This blocks the AIDS virus from attaching to these receptors, preventing the virus from getting a foothold.

Robert Gallo, one of the original discoverers of HIV, also found a related virus which he named HTLV-I. HTLV-I causes cancer. Gallo says that there is enough similarity between the varying HIV viruses to develop a blood test for them all. He is hopeful that these similarities mean that a vaccine will be able to be developed to protect individuals against AIDS.

All of the research to fight the AIDS virus has so far offered few positive results. Today, there is no vaccine to prevent AIDS, no cure for AIDS, and the result of contracting the virus may be 100 percent fatal. The best protection against contracting the disease is having an awareness of the disease and how it is spread, and then taking appropriate steps to protect yourself from exposure.

Today, in spite of major advances in medicine, science, and technology, the war against disease goes on. As Jenner probed the unknown to find a miraculous cure for smallpox, so do researchers today do the same in attempting to conquer AIDS. As Pasteur methodically and scientifically plodded against anthrax and rabies, so do genetic engineers attempt to conquer cancer. No doubt, in time, today's scientists' efforts will prove to be successful, and then we shall move on to the fight against the next new disease to afflict humankind.

GLOSSARY

Abiogenesis. See *Spontaneous Generation.*

Acquired immune deficiency syndrome (AIDS). An immunodeficiency disease caused by a retrovirus called human immunodeficiency virus (HIV). Earlier designations for this virus were: (American) human T-cell leukemia (later called lymphotropic) virus (HTLV-III); and (French) lymphadenopathy virus (LAV).

Active acquired immunity. Immunity acquired by sensitization to the immune system by an antigen. The T and B memory cells remain in the blood. In case of another attack, the T and B cells respond quickly to prevent reinfection.

Agglutinate. To clump.

AIDS. See *Acquired immune deficiency syndrome.*

Allergens. Antigens that trigger an allergic reaction.

Allergy. Extreme sensitivity to certain substances, such as particular kinds of pollen, food, hair, or cloth. Asthma, hay fever, headaches, and hives are common signs of allergy.

Antibody. A protein molecule that an organism produces in response to stimulation by an antigen and is capable of combining specifically with that antigen.

Antigen. A molecule which, when introduced into an organism, is able to stimulate the production of antibodies capable of interacting with it.

Antitoxin. Any substance capable of neutralizing a toxin.

Arachidonic acid. A chemical produced during allergic reactions.

Attenuated. Weakened.

Autoimmune. The breakdown of the immune system's tolerance to itself; when a person's body develops an immune response to its own antigens.

Azidothymidine (AZT). A drug used to help relieve the symptoms of some AIDS victims.

B cell. A lymphocyte that is thought to mature in the bone marrow; a major cell in the immune response that produces antibody molecules.

Bacteria (singular, bacterium). A kingdom of unicellular organisms without a true nucleus that are capable of stimulating the immune response.

Bacteriophage. A virus that attacks bacteria.

Basophile. A cell or tissue that is readily stained with basic dyes.

Biologic. Of the nature of living matter.

Causative agent. The pathogen that causes a disease or the immune response; for example, HIV is the causative agent of AIDS.

Cellular immunity. That part of the immune system that is primarily related to a cellular response to antigenic stimulus; as opposed to *humoral immunity.*

Chemotherapy. Treatment of a disease with chemicals.

Chromosomes. Strands of DNA found in the nucleus of cells; responsible for the inheritance of higher organisms.

Clone. All the progeny of a cell throughout many cell divisions.

Contagious. Able to be spread from one individual to another.

Cowpox. A virus, similar to smallpox, that produces a mild infection in cows and humans.

Deoxyribonucleic acid (DNA). The stuff genes are made of; found in chromosomes.

DNA. See *Deoxyribonucleic acid.*

Effector function. Response to a stimulus.

Epidemiology. Science that studies the distribution of disease in human populations.

Erythrocytes. Red blood cells containing hemoglobin; they carry oxygen from the lungs to all the body cells.

Filament. A thread; a fiber.

Gamma interferon. A chemical produced by T cells, which is being synthesized and used as an experimental drug in fighting cancer.

Gene. Concentrations of DNA. Genes carry the individual's inherited traits, i.e., eye color, hair color, and the like.

Gene splicing. A technique developed by genetic engineers to place foreign genes into a virus.

Genetic engineering. The experimental field in genetics and immunology in which scientists are working on gene splicing and other techniques to alter inheritance and fight disease.

Germ theory of disease. The theory that all forms of disease are caused by microscopic foreign organisms, which are called pathogens.

Hapten. A chemical that is capable of combining with an antibody molecule. A hapten is incapable of stimulating the immune response unless it is chemically united with an antigen.

Histamine. A chemical produced by cells during allergic reactions. This chemical dilates blood vessels, causing inflammation.

HIV. See *human immunodeficiency virus.*

Human immunodeficiency virus (HIV). The cause of AIDS. Previously called: (in the United States) human T-cell leukemia (later lymphotropic) virus III (HTLV-III); and (in France) lymphadenopathy virus (LAV).

Humoral immunity. That part of the immune system that is primarily related to a molecular response to antigens, as opposed to *cellular immunity.*

Hybridoma. The cell resulting from fusion of a cancer (myeloma) cell with a lymphocyte.

Immune. Resistant to disease or infection.

Immune-deficiency disease. Any disease in which the immune response does not function.

Immune response. The most powerful body defense against invasion by a pathogen; all of the body defenses, both cellular and humoral, attacking a foreign invader.

Immunoglobulins. Protein molecules which possess antibody activity; classified as Ig molecules: IgG, IgA, IgM, IgD, and IgF.

Immunosuppressants. Any drugs that suppress the action of the immune system.

Inoculate. To introduce an antigen into an organism in order to immunize, cure, or experiment.

In vitro. Refers to "in glass" or "in the test tube."

Killed vaccine. Any vaccine made up of a killed pathogen.

LAK cells. Lymphokine-activated killer cells.

Lesion. An injury or other alteration of any organ or tissue resulting in damage, injury, or loss of function.

Leukocytes. Another term for white blood cells.

Live vaccine. Any vaccine made up of a weakened form of a live pathogen.

Lymphocytes. A class of white blood cells; part of the immune response.

Macrophage. A large phagocyte.

Mast cell. A connective tissue cell.

Microbe. Any living thing that is too small to be seen with the naked eye.

Microbiology. The science that studies microscopic organisms.

Microorganism. Any organism of microscopic size, i.e., bacteria, virus.

Monoclonal antibodies. Antibody produced by a cell that is formed by fusing an antibody-producing cell of limited viability with a malignant (cancerous) cell. This fusion produces a hybrid cell called a *hybridoma.* The progeny of the hybridoma cell, called a clone and considered to be immortal, may produce a specific monoclonal antibody.

Nonself. Anything not of self; refers to foreign cells, tissues, or particles that enter the body.

Opsonins. Antibodies that aid in the process of *phagocytosis.*

Organic. Living or derived from living things.

Organism. Any living thing.

Passive acquired immunity. When a person is not manufacturing his or her own antibodies, as in the newborn (maternal antibodies) or in immune serum therapy.

Pathogen. Any disease-causing organism.

Phagocytes. Also called macrophages; white blood cells that ingest microorganisms; cell eaters.

Phagocytosis. The process of one cell engulfing (eating) another cell.

Plasma cell. A mature antibody-producing cell derived from a *B cell.*

Protein. A large organic compound containing amino acids as its basic structural units; coded for by a specific gene.

Pure culture. A culture of an organism free of all other foreign matter; obtained under *sterile* conditions.

Receptors. Found on antibodies; allows the antibody to match up with a given antigen.

Retrovirus. An organism that reproduces by making its own genetic material within the cell it infects.

Self. Refers to an individual's own antigens.

Serotherapy. A technique for inducing passive immunity through one or more injections of serum that contain antibodies against a given disease.

Serum. The body liquid in which blood cells are suspended.

Side-chain theory. Theory stating that blood antibodies produce side chains of proteins in response to specific antigens.

Specificity. The ability of an antibody to be specific to one antigen.

Spontaneous generation (Abiogenesis). The belief that living organisms can be produced from nonliving matter or decomposing *organic* matter.

Sterile. Free from bacteria and other foreign microorganisms.

Steroid. A specific class of hormones; some are used to reduce inflammation; others are involved in sexual differentiation.

Systemic. Affecting the whole body.

T cell. A lymphocyte that is thought to be produced in the thymus gland; helps kill pathogens; regulates the production of B cells.

Toxin. A poison; specifically, an organic poison capable of producing an antitoxin reaction.

Vaccinate. To inoculate with a vaccine in order to produce immunity.

Vaccine. A suspension of a killed or attenuated live pathogen which, when inoculated, is capable of stimulating antibody production.

Vaccinia. The cowpox virus which was used in Jenner's vaccine.

Variolation. An early attempt at immunization against smallpox via inoculation of a healthy person with fluid from the lesions of a person with smallpox.

Vector. A disease carrier; for example, mosquitoes are insect vectors of malaria, carrying the pathogens from one host to another.

Virulent. Poisonous or harmful.

Virus. A submicroscopic pathogen having the ability to reproduce inside a living cell.

Zidovudene. Generic name for AZT.

CHRONOLOGY OF MAJOR CONTRIBUTIONS

Thucydides	460?–400? B.C.E.	First to recognize immunity in persons who had had a disease and recovered.
Mithridates	120?–63 B.C.E.	First attempt to induce immunity to poisons (supposed).
Athanasius Kircher	1601–1680	One of the first to make connection between microorganisms and their causation of disease.
Giovar Cosimo Bonomo	1666–1696	Linked mites to the cause of the disease scabies.
Antonie van Leeuwenhoek	1632–1723	First to see bacteria under microscope.
Jan Baptista van Helmont	1580–1644	Put forward a recipe for the spontaneous generation of mice from grain.

Francesco Redi	1626–1697	First to refute theory of spontaneous generation with hard, scientific evidence.
John Needham	1713–1781	Presented a scientific paper stating that microorganisms arose spontaneously from spoiled broth.
Lazzaro Spallanzani	1729–1799	Refuted Needham's findings. Stated that the theory of spontaneous generation was in error.
Edward Jenner	1749–1823	Discovered vaccination (active immunization) as a method of prevention against the spread of smallpox.
Louis Pasteur	1822–1895	Father of immunology and founder of the science of microbiology. Disproved theory of spontaneous generation. Discovered that microbes cause wine to spoil, and suggested a process of heating (pasteurization) to kill them. Found method for preventing spread of pébrine, a disease that affects silkworms. Developed true germ theory of disease. Discovered cause of chicken cholera and methods for prevention. Discovered cause and methods for preventing anthrax in sheep. Developed vaccine for the cure of rabies.
Joseph Lister	1827–1912	Developed aseptic methods for surgery and childbirth.
Armaur Hanser	1841–1912	Discovered leprosy bacillus.
William Budd	1811–1880	Worked on typhoid fever.

Robert Koch	1843–1910	Developed technique for obtaining pure cultures on sterile media. Also discovered the causative organisms for tuberculosis and for cholera. His method for developing pure cultures became known as Koch's postulates.
Émile Roux	1853–1933	Discovered the bacterial toxin of the diphtheria virus.
Alexandre Yersin	1863–1943	Along with Roux, discovered the bacterial toxin of the diphtheria virus.
Emil von Behring	1854–1917	Worked on theory of antibody production. Coined term "antibody" and classified an antibody's functions. Discovered diphtheria antitoxin.
Shibasaburo Kitasato	1852–1931	Worked with von Behring on antibody theories; also classified functions of antibodies.
Élie Metchnikoff	1845–1916	Chief proponent of the cellular theory (phagocyte theory).
George H. F. Nuttall	1862–1937	First to introduce humoral theory.
Richard F. J. Pfeiffer	1858–1945	Demonstrated that blood serum destroys pathogens. Developed Pfeiffer's phenomenon and law.
Paul Ehrlich	1854–1915	Developed technique for staining the tubercular bacillus. Worked with poisons ricin and abrin, and demonstrated that animals could be made immune to poisons through inoculation. Demonstrated that a child obtains

passive acquired immunity from the mother. Investigated how drugs can be used to kill pathogens; father of chemotherapy. A chief proponent of humoral theory of immunity.

Michael C. Heidelberger	1890s	First to identify immunoglobulins (Ig molecules).
W. M. W. Haffkine	(1860–1930)	Worked with attenuated vaccines for protective immunization. Developed the killed vaccine to induce active acquired immunity. First to apply prophylactic immunization to people.
H. B. Maitland	1920s	Demonstrated that it was possible to grow a virus on kidney cells that are not dividing.
Ernest William Goodpasture	1886–1960	Developed accepted method for using fertilized hen egg to cultivate viruses.
Ladislaus Laszio Marton	1941	Introduced the practical use of the electron microscope for studying viruses and other microscopic phenomena.
John Franklin Enders	1897–1985	Demonstrated that poliomyelitis virus could be grown on monkey kidneys. Isolated and typed three strains of polio virus, thus setting the stage for the development of vaccines for viruses.
Macfarlane Burnet	1899–1985	Developed clonal selection theory.
Enzo Paoletti	1987	Used genetic engineering to make a new kind of vaccine.

107

Kimishige Ishizaka and Teruko Ishizaka	1966	Discovered IgE molecule is responsible for a majority of allergic reactions.
Ray Patterson	1986–1987	Developed a new series of allergy shots that require fewer injections.
Lawrence Lichtenstein	1986–1987	Discovered that arachidonic acid is the major component of allergic reactions.

INDEX